PENGUIN PASSNOTES

Cider with Rosie

Peter J. Connor was educated at Le[...]
University where he read English an[...]
Philosophy. After working abroad fo[...]
took his Postgraduate Certificate of [...]
Manchester. He has taught at variou[...]
colleges in London and has also written the study
guide to *Henry IV, Part 1* and *The War of the
Worlds* in the Passnotes series.

PENGUIN PASSNOTES

LAURIE LEE

Cider with Rosie

PETER J. CONNOR
ADVISORY EDITOR: STEPHEN COOTE, M.A., PH.D.

PENGUIN BOOKS

Penguin Books Ltd, Harmondsworth, Middlesex, England
Viking Penguin Inc., 40 West 23rd Street, New York, New York 10010, U.S.A.
Penguin Books Australia Ltd, Ringwood, Victoria, Australia
Penguin Books Canada Limited, 2801 John Street, Markham, Ontario, Canada L3R 1B4
Penguin Books (N.Z.) Ltd, 182–190 Wairau Road, Auckland 10, New Zealand

First published 1985
Reprinted 1986 (twice)

Made and printed in Great Britain by
Richard Clay Ltd, Bungay, Suffolk
Typeset in Monophoto Ehrhardt

*The publishers are grateful to the Associated Examining Board and to
the University of Oxford Delegacy of Local Examinations for permission
to reproduce questions from examination papers used in this book.*

*The Examination Boards accept no responsibility whatsoever for the accuracy
or method of working in any suggested answers given as models.*

Contents

To the Student

This book is designed to help you with your O-level or C.S.E. English Literature examination. It contains a synopsis of the plot, a glossary of the more unfamiliar words and phrases, and a commentary on some of the issues raised by the text. An account of the writer's life is also included for background.

Page references in parentheses are to the Penguin edition.

When you use this book remember that it is no more than an aid to your study. It will help you find passages quickly and perhaps give you some ideas for essays. But remember: *This book is not a substitute for reading the text and it is your knowledge and your response that matter.* These are the things the examiners are looking for, and they are also the things that will give you the most pleasure. Show your knowledge and appreciation to the examiner, and show them clearly.

Introduction: Laurie Lee and Cider with Rosie

Cider with Rosie is a delightful picture of a boy's growing up and finding his vocation as a poet, set in the lost world of the pre-war English countryside. With great acuteness of observation, humour, sensitivity and richness of language, Laurie Lee evokes this world of childhood and adolescence: the sights, sounds and smells of the countryside, the odd characters and deep feelings that characterize it. The book is a classic evocation of a lost and beautiful era.

Cider with Rosie is based on Laurie Lee's own life. In reading it, one is aware that it is the work of a born poet, of a man who delights in using the English language in all its power and beauty. Laurie Lee was born in Gloucestershire and educated locally. *Cider with Rosie* describes the early years of his life, and its sequel, *As I Walked Out One Midsummer Morning*, describes a journey he later made on foot through Spain where he was trapped by the outbreak of the Spanish Civil War.

It is obvious from *Cider with Rosie* that Laurie Lee has not only a poet's wealth of evocative words to describe the world about him, but that he also has a lively sense of humour. Between 1950 and 1951 he was made Curator of Eccentricities for the Festival of Britain. The following year he was awarded the M.B.E. Laurie Lee has written a number of books of poetry and you will no doubt be familiar with his poetry from anthologies you have read at school. He is also a writer of excellent travel books and is a great lover of music.

First published in 1959, *Cider with Rosie* has established itself as one of the classics of English country life. It takes its place beside such books as Flora Thompson's *Larkrise to Candleford* and Thomas Hardy's *The Woodlanders*.

Synopsis of Cider with Rosie

Cider with Rosie does not have a complicated plot. Rather is it a book whose thirteen chapters describe various aspects of life in the English countryside before the Second World War, and the stages and experiences of the author's growing to manhood. The first chapter describes the arrival of the three-year-old Laurie Lee in a secluded country village. We are introduced to his mother and, with great skill, to the vivid but bewildering experiences of early childhood.

The second chapter develops the picture of maternal love and the fearful nature of the outside world. A number of bizarre experiences are recounted, including those of Jones's goat and the story of a suicide. The chapter also contains strong elements of comedy.

Chapter three is a far from sentimental account of life in the village primary school, of Laurie Lee's fellow pupils and of the various and sometimes spiteful characters of his teachers.

Chapter four returns us to the safe world of home and describes the life of a large, natural and vigorous family. We also see the birth of Laurie's interest in music.

The fifth chapter introduces us to some remarkable characters: the two eccentric 'grannies', wonderfully described through the language they employ, their superstitions and dignity as they approach the ends of their lives.

The sixth chapter is more sombre in its descriptions of violence, suicide and death. It is both strong and dignified.

The seventh chapter is a complex but loving portrait of the author's mother, her past, her quick and unpredictable changes of mood, her delicate feelings and the loneliness of her life without a husband.

By way of contrast, chapter eight describes the sports and pastimes of the varying country seasons.

Chapter nine concerns illness, in this case the rather serious childhood fevers to which the young Laurie was prone. We are made to realize the vulnerability of country people to disease in the days before modern advances in medicine.

The narrator's uncles, described in chapter ten, are the heroes of Laurie's fatherless childhood. We hear of adventurous pasts and of a world of excitement outside the secluded village.

Chapter eleven describes some of the communal celebrations enjoyed by the village, and we have a delightful feeling of shared, happy, slightly excessive, country life.

The twelfth chapter, 'First Bite at the Apple', contains the experiences which give the book its title. It is a subtle, comic and moving picture of an adolescent boy's growing awareness of girls. We see Laurie's awakening interest in girls; the physical changes of adolescence which give him a new lease of energy; and then, in a scene which produces some of the finest poetry in the book, we have the description of Laurie's liaison with Rosie, of his fear, her enthusiasm and his final acceptance of his feelings.

The final chapter of *Cider with Rosie*, 'Last Days', movingly evokes the end of the rural life that Laurie knew. We read of motor cars, of the break-up of the family and of the responsibilities of a more adult life. We see also how the old social structure of the village begins to crumble. Finally, we see how Laurie, now a young man, begins to think more seriously about girls and about becoming a poet. We leave him on the threshold of manhood, with the old world in which he grew up slowly passing into history.

An Account of the Story

Chapter 1: 'FIRST LIGHT', *pp. 9–24*

The opening chapter of the book begins with the abrupt and bewildering arrival of the young Laurie Lee in Slad, the village where he is to spend his childhood.

The chapter presents most of the important themes which are later developed, and introduces us immediately to a quality of writing which is sustained throughout the book. The title, 'First Light', suggests that we are to witness the child's awakening as he discovers the people and the world around him.

The distress of the three-year-old child is conveyed by both a sensuous and concrete imagery in which Lee describes how he is almost swallowed up by the long grass, and the heat and the smells of his new home. He feels bewildered and alone in a strange, new world. He is rescued by his sisters, the guardian angels of his childhood; boisterous but comforting, they carry him off to the cottage where they are to live.

All this happens towards the end of the First World War, a fact we must bear in mind throughout this recollection of a vanished age.

The cottage is a strange mixture of squalor and beauty, simultaneously rotting and blooming. The author remembers his arrival there as his real birth, his true introduction to life. The chaos of arrival is described and the vivacity of the sisters conveyed in the description of them stripping the fruit bushes in the garden.

We catch our first glimpse of the author's mother, a central figure in the book, as she bustles to and fro decorating the cottage with garden flowers. We get a child's-eye view of the furnishing of the cottage with a clutter of objects from the past.

Finally, order is established and the furnishing is over. The atmosphere, the 'tradition', of the house is fixed for the next twenty years.

Laurie begins to discover a wider world as he becomes more mobile with his 'new tricks of dressing and getting about'. Life is a series of experiments in which everything is of consuming interest. Using the metaphor of an adventurer mapping unknown country, the author describes his exploration of the cottage's surroundings and his discovery of, and delight in, the 'well-prodded horrors' he finds. These 'horrors' give him his first glimpse of a 'destroying force' (p. 14).

Again using an extended metaphor, he remembers his mother and sisters as great ships sailing majestically through the house.

He discovers the magic of water in the scullery, an important room. Here the washing of clothes, bodies and food takes place, all three activities dominated by the figure of his mother.

Food, too, is another of Laurie's preoccupations. Vegetables are stolen and eaten raw; pastry is devoured; huge meals are cooked in vast cauldrons; great quantities of bread are delivered and eaten while still warm, and sometimes strange objects are discovered within them.

The story of Laurie waking up and believing himself to be blind (pp. 16, 17) introduces us to the lively, colloquial speech of the Lee children. When his sisters clear his eyes, Laurie is amazed by the colours of the trees outside his window. He learns that it is autumn, and this discovery of change and decay upsets him, but he is soon distracted by Marjorie's excited announcement that ''''e's turned up again!''' This is an army deserter who lives in the woods. He is a man who, to the young Laurie, seems to be something that actually grows in the ground, 'a conglomeration of woody things'. His appearance reminds Laurie of his uncles, all of them in the war, and their exciting stories. Laurie wonders if the man had 'lost the war in the woods' and realizes he has when one day he hears that the police have taken him away.

In the winter, another new experience for Laurie, his mother goes away to visit the absent father, a peripheral figure throughout the book. His mother leaves the girls in charge, 'tumbling ... arguing, quarrelling ...'. Disorder returns – the house becomes filthy and meals are almost inedible. Laurie seizes his chance of freedom, wandering far afield and avidly collecting new objects and experiences. The sisters are characterized by their different reactions to this chaos: Doth giggling, Phyl weeping and Marjorie exhausted and resigned.

Laurie is not surprised to hear of what he thinks is the end of the world as he hears the girls discussing the Armistice. All the children go down to the village to witness the celebrations. In appalled fascination, they see the school catch fire and blaze 'as if the sight had been saved for [that] day'.

Laurie is overcome with doubts about the future, his uncles and his father. With his mother absent as well, his insecurity leads him to expect an end to his own life and to the end of the world.

The first chapter thus evokes, by rich use of language, the fears and joys of early childhood. Briefly, but sharply, Laurie Lee touches on nearly all of the themes which are developed later in the book, telling the reader just enough to engage his attention while withholding enough to maintain his curiosity.

Chapter 2: 'FIRST NAMES', *pp. 25–40*

Just as the end of the war had bewildered Laurie, so the peace that follows has no clear meaning for him. His mother returns with tales of riotous rejoicing, demobbed soldiers pass the time in the village, but Laurie can see no change in his own life; he returns to 'burrowing among the mysteries of indoors and out' (p. 25). His lively curiosity is conveyed by the descriptive verbs the author employs to explain the fascination of all the new objects that surround the child in the house.

The fact that there remained 'the eternal comfort of the women' leads into the story of Laurie's banishment from his mother's bed, the incident which first alerts him to 'the merciless rejection of women' (p. 28).

The author conveys, with use of almost luxurious imagery, the comfort, warmth and privilege of sleeping in his mother's bed. After he is tricked into leaving her, he feels a sense of betrayal that marks the end of an era in his life; he grows '... a little tougher, a little colder ...' (p. 28) and his attention turns more to the outside world.

Here childhood fears take the shape of imaginary monsters marching towards the house and of the 'Old Men', the spiteful phantoms his sisters use to frighten the boys into submission – the perfect substitutes for the absent father's authority.

We next hear the story of Jones's goat, a 'real old pagan of flesh and blood'. This anecdote is skilfully told, keeping us in suspense as to the nature of the monster until the comic anticlimax. The story serves to illustrate the sometimes hysterical excitement which prevails in the Lee household and also emphasizes the credulous, magical atmosphere of the village at that time. The beast itself is described as a mythical being immensely potent and majestic in the moonlight. To Laurie, though, Jones's goat seems 'a natural phenomenon of that time, part of a village that cast up beasts and spirits as casually as human beings' (p. 32). This acceptance of the bizarre and the supernatural is illustrated in a series of anecdotes.

The Two-Headed Sheep, the Bulls Cross Coach and Hangman's House all show the power of folk-memories in an isolated area as yet almost untouched by modern industrial civilization. These stories all contain incidents and images which are important to the village people. The tragedy of Bulls Cross Coach – 'that small but local disaster' (p. 33) – still has an immediacy which appals people more than the mass slaughter of the Great War.

The story of the hangman's suicide after executing his own son is a powerful tale, contrasting with the boys' untroubled playing in his dark and decaying cottage.

The character studies of village eccentrics also help to convey the humour and strangeness of the village's atmosphere. We also note that making the acquaintance of these characters marks another step in Laurie's development; he is now five years old and beginning to be aware of the existence of other people. All of these various and colourful eccentrics are drawn with great vividness by the adult author. Faces, mannerisms and speech are all given in telling detail.

Charlie's mock-heroic feats of arms are amusingly recounted and the description of him resembling 'a land-locked Viking' (p. 35) is a memorable and informative image.

Albert, too, is precisely captured in a few strokes of the pen. His 'black beetle's body' and 'soft-boiled eyes' are arresting images which surprise and enlighten us. The village's fear of his supposed powers is made funny to us, yet he is not made to seem ridiculous.

The description of the smelly Willy the Fish as 'loose-lipped' and 'sad-eyed' (p. 36) neatly and concisely expresses both his physical appearance and emotional state. The brief story is all the more humorous for its punchy last phrase: 'the truth was poor Willy stank' (p. 36).

John-Jack, mentioned only in passing, is another who gives us further evidence of the village's isolation. One can hardly imagine anyone today, even in the remotest area, being left alone long enough to produce five children from an incestuous relationship.

Strangest and most comic of all, perhaps, is the gentle Emmanuel Twinning who wears blankets and shares his house with his skewbald horse.

The final section of this chapter recounts in comic detail a domestic crisis. After a long drought the heavens open in the middle of the night. Laurie's mother is possessed by hysterical fear, '"It's coming in! Get up or we'll be drowned!"' (p. 38). The cottage stands in the path of the floods; everyone is called in to help avert disaster. The panic and breathless activity are conveyed in prose that speeds on, with barely a pause for the reader to get his breath. Through it all the figure of Laurie's mother dominates, hysterical, protective and ranting against the injustice of it all. It was only much later, says Laurie Lee, that he realized there was little chance of a flood. His mother's 'frenzies and scares belonged to something else altogether' – perhaps her resentment about her husband's abandonment of his family.

Chapter 3: 'VILLAGE SCHOOL', *pp. 41–59*

The opening paragraphs of the chapter describe further the valley in which Laurie is brought up. We learn that it was a small community, cut off from the wider world. Laurie Lee likens it to 'living in a bean-pod; one could see nothing but the bed one lay in' (p. 41).

Water and light predominate. The rain comes in from the west, drenching men, animals and earth while the light creates magical effects of shade in the grass and trees.

The villagers have three ways of earning a living; farming, working in the cloth-mills at the nearest town – Stroud – or working for the Squire. The village has all the necessary amenities, but no more.

The main part of the chapter is taken up with the village school, a single building catering for all children up to the age of fourteen and run by a headmistress with a younger assistant. The teaching is indiscriminate: 'a few memories, a jumbled list of wars, and a dreary image of the world's geography' (p. 42).

Through the various anecdotes in this chapter we learn more about the author himself, his family and the curious assortment of children in the valley.

'Loll', as his family call him, is most reluctant to begin school. However, he has no choice but to give in, and the author describes vividly the confusion of his first day when 'the playground roared like a rodeo' (p. 43), a scene which must strike a chord in anybody who can remember going to school for the first time.

Soon, though, he learns the techniques of survival: '. . . I felt like a veteran and grew as ruthless as anyone' (p. 44). New toys and objects engage his interest and he is captivated by the sixteen-year-old assistant teacher.

Loll's childish candour leads to an amusing incident with the 'opulent widow' who replaces the 'beautiful assistant'. In an effort to convince him that she is not wearing a wig she says, 'If only you could watch me getting dressed in the morning . . .' (p. 45). Loll's imagination is 'stirred'. The suggestion of female secrets is explored later in the book.

The Infants' room is 'a brief but cosy anarchy', in which the children 'exhaled [their] last guiltless days' (p. 45). At Loll's desk sit Poppy and Jo, two girls 'whose names and bodies were to distract and haunt' him for the next fifteen years of his life (p. 45). Another girl, Vera, is the unwitting cause of Loll's first 'public shock'. With an air of scientific detachment he whacks her on the head with a stick – 'without spite or passion' – and then leaves her 'to try something else'.

His experiment leads to a ticking-off in the 'Big Room', his first taste of the unpleasant consequences certain actions can have.

The author's brother Jack is described as something of a prodigy. Quiet and studious, he is quickly promoted to the Big Room. In contrast, the author describes himself as 'a natural Infant', happy to do as the others, 'the fat lord' of his nursery life (p. 48). Soon, too soon for his liking, he has to move up to the Big Room. Here he finds 'a world both adult and tough' (p. 48), without the innocence of the Infants' room. Now he has to struggle, make friends, and fight for a place near the stove, 'a symbol of caste' among the pupils (p. 48).

Even the different teacher marks the change from innocence to experience. Instead of the comforting warmth of the young assistant teacher, there is now the predatory Miss B, 'as physically soothing as a rake' (p. 49). Crabby, as the children call her, is the epitome of the short-tempered and spiteful school-teacher. She is at the centre of one of the most memorable incidents in the book. Her mannerisms are described in such a way as to make us feel as antagonistic towards her as do the school children themselves. To the author she seemed 'a natural manifestation of what we expected of school' (p. 50), a school which seemed designed merely to keep the children from the fields and woods where they longed to be. In describing the smells and sounds of the first warm days, Laurie Lee conveys the children's desire to be free.

At last the rebellion comes, led by a most unlikely hero: the pudding-like Spadge Hopkins. His defiance of, and victory over, Crabby is the outcome of long taunting and an unbearable desire to be away and free.

Crabby is replaced by the more effective Miss Wardley. She calls the author 'Fat-and-Lazy', due to his habit of falling asleep at his desk in the afternoons, and often sends him out because of his refusal to blow his nose.

Both the author's brothers are now at school. Jack is still 'the accepted genius', and is left to his own devices. Tony, the youngest, neither learns nor obeys. He has an 'outrageous cheekiness' that protects him from retribution. Loll only wins Miss Wardley's approval by writing faked essays on otters. School, though, eventually becomes pleasurable: '... in the end I relished it' (p. 53). The author describes the rote-learning and some abiding images of his school days: decorations, the strange admixture of children, Miss Wardley at her 'high desk throne'.

He recounts one of his recurring childhood fantasies, that he is the last son of a king, then tells of his return to the classroom where he makes an offering of his work to the bully Walt Kerry. In the playground the boys punch and play, and then make a trip to 'the girls' own place', mysterious and comic. The intensity of these memories is marked by the change from past to present tense, emphasizing their clarity and power.

We learn also of the author's early gift for writing poetry: 'one wrote a dozen an hour, one simply didn't hesitate'.

He tells of the routine of school life; the teachers' reproaches, the lame excuses, the tricks for taking a day off or avoiding tests. What they learned, he says, were 'the less formal truths – the names of flowers, the habits of birds . . . the treacherous innocence of boys, the shy charm of girls . . .' (p. 57).

Their 'inborn hatred for freaks and outcasts [is] tempered by meeting them daily'. Nick and Edna, the children of the brother and sister mentioned in the previous chapter, and Rosso the gipsy boy, engage the children's sympathies and enlarge their understanding.

But school was 'just a conveyor belt along which the short years drew [them]' (p. 58). The children become older, adopt superior airs and graces, and wait for that 'lucky, lucky point of time' when they can leave. When they do, they never return.

Chapter 4: 'THE KITCHEN', *pp. 60–77*

From the outside world of the school and its strange characters, the author returns to the evocation of his home and of domestic life.

He begins by emphasizing the power of home life, both physical and emotional, that has lasted into adult life and manifests itself in dreams. Apart from the physical circumstances of the dilapidated cottage, the most important factor is 'the rule of women'

We learn that Laurie's father left the family when the author was three, to return only on fleeting visits. We learn of his feckless but ambitious youth, and of his tangled marital affairs. Thus, we discover that the girls are really the author's half-sisters (by his father's first marriage) and that only Jack and Tony are his full brothers. While raising this brood, his mother still believes in the eventual return of her husband.

The author, though, is 'perfectly content in this world of women' (p. 61) with its excess of warmth and attention from mother and half-sisters. The eldest girl, Marjorie, is 'dreamily gentle', a blonde beauty of reassuring calmness. Dorothy is more volatile, 'a perilous firework', energetic and much given to outrageous gossip and high spirits. The youngest, Phyllis, is 'an unclassified solitary', separate from her older sisters. Her favourite task is to put the boys to bed, when she displays a warm tenderness the author vividly remembers.

The only half-brother at home is Harold. The thin, bony, unhappy boy stands apart from the others, perhaps because of his love for his absent father (p. 63). Of the author's true brothers, Jack is the eldest and sharpest, as we have already learned from the previous chapter. He is also the author's 'close companion', with whom he shares a bed, quarrels and plays. Tony, the youngest, is considered, like Phyllis among her sisters, to be the odd one out among the boys. He is also more contemplative, 'a brooding, imaginative solitary', with strange and incomprehensible gifts, who seems always to be either alone or struggling to keep up with his brothers.

The cottage, then, has a population of eight. They are crammed into its three floors, with people passing through others' bedrooms to get to their beds. During the day the kitchen is the centre of family life. Here everybody jostles in 'a family fug' (p. 64). The room is filled with a higgledy-piggledy collection of bric-à-brac and ancient furniture. It seems typical of its character that the harmonium is for coats and the piano 'for dust and photographs'.

The rest of this chapter is taken up by a description of a typical family day. Laurie and Jack wake, dress and bicker before going down to the kitchen for breakfast. There they find 'the morning muddle': the youngest boy cutting bread with a ruler, the cat eating the butter.

Eventually, porridge is served. The girls eat 'moonishly', still sleepy and absorbed in their night-time reveries, until they suddenly realize how late it is and rush off to work, Marjorie and Phyllis to shops and Dorothy to the cloth-mill.

The boys are now on their own. In the holidays they go off to play or to find scraps of food, for they are always hungry. Holidays, though, are a time of risk; at any moment the boys might be called to do an errand for their mother, who constantly seems to be running out of essential supplies. The task usually falls to Laurie, since his brother Jack makes 'his sly get-away as usual' (p. 69). For Jack is 'jumpy, shifty, and quick-off-the-mark', not at all like his brothers. His 'speed and guile' are shown by the way he eats. Eight hungry mouths and the mother's haphazard method of serving do not prevent Jack from wolfing down plate after plate of the 'heavy brown mash' of lentil stew that is the family's staple diet. Since 'there [is] never quite enough to go round', the others are necessarily left hungry. To this day, says the author, he still has the scar of 'a twisted, food-crazed nature' which has him calling for food in the middle of the night . . .

At the end of the day the boys return to the 'smoky comfort' of the kitchen, where their mother is cooking. The only light is from the fire, which casts 'convulsive' shadows. The boys light candles and then the iron table-lamp. But all these sources produce only pools of light and 'the kitchen [remains] mostly in shadow' (p. 71). Laurie takes up his violin for his nightly practice. He sets to enthusiastically, hoping for the reward of his mother's glances of 'piercing, anxious encouragement' when he gets a note right. Her enjoyment seems to rejuvenate her and it is to gain her approval that Laurie plays.

At the same time Jack clears a space for his 'inscrutable homework', while Tony plays with the cat. Their mother eats tea standing up, her attention fixed on the fire, which it is essential to keep going.

After tea, the boys settle around the lamp. Laurie draws, Jack continues his homework and Tony plays with cotton reels and mutters the story he is making up.

The evening calm is broken by the arrival of the girls, back from work. When they have eaten their supper, they too settle down to their own tasks in the lamplight. Evening becomes night and in the 'rosy darkness' of the kitchen Laurie becomes drowsy, half-hearing snatches of the girls' stories. Eventually, the girls carry him upstairs, undress him and put him to bed with Jack.

Chapter 5: 'GRANNIES IN THE WAINSCOT', *pp. 78–94*

Two of the most memorable eccentrics in *Cider with Rosie* are focused upon in this chapter. As the title suggests, Granny Trill and Granny Wallon live very close to the Lees; it is almost as if they are two mice behind the wainscot.

The opening paragraph of the chapter describes the house and its history. It is now in a dilapidated state, a rambling building with a T-shape, in the top-stroke of which live the two old grannies, one above the other.

Granny Trill and Granny Wallon are 'rival ancients' (p. 78) who live 'on each other's nerves'. As we shall see, it is only their 'perpetual enmity' which keeps them alive. To the young Laurie their old and decrepit bodies are those of witches. They never speak to each other, preferring to communicate by banging on the floor or ceiling, and refer to each other as ''Er-Down-Under' and ''Er-Up-Atop'.

The former, who lives on the same level of the cottage as the Lees, is Granny Wallon. She is 'a tiny white shrew', gossiping and energetic, with a 'crisp and trotting body' (p. 79). There are 'rumours of noble blood' in her mysterious past. Now, though, she is very poor. But she is celebrated in the village for her homemade wines.

Making wine occupies most of her time throughout the year. First, in April, she collects the ingredients. She scours the countryside and returns home in the evening laden with produce, until she has 'buckets of cowslips, dandelions, elder-blossom crammed into every corner of the house' (p. 79). To Laurie, all these ingredients are a dizzying brew of sights and smells. Into her pots and vats goes just about anything: 'Granny Wallon made wine as though demented, out of anything at all' (p. 79). When, after a long wait, the wine is ready to be drunk, the old lady, 'wispily grinning,' appears at the Lees' window with a sample jug. Though the wine seems innocuous enough, the whole family is soon tipsy. Content with the result, Granny Wallon goes back to her own kitchen.

If Granny Wallon is a 'shrew', then ''Er-Up-Atop', Granny Trill, is 'as frugal as a sparrow and as simple in her ways as a grub' (p. 82). She sits for hours oblivious in her chair with only 'the gentle motion of her jaws' betraying the fact that she is alive. Her curious timetable – rising at four in the morning and returning to bed at five in the afternoon – seems to bear the traces of her early years living in the woods with her woodcutter father. Granny Trill's door is always open and the children are frequent visitors. On a typical visit they find her patiently combing her sparse white hair. The children innocently taunt her for her baldness. She seems to take no notice, but suddenly leaps up and starts screaming that she has more hair than ''Er down there' (p. 83). Then, just as suddenly, her anger subsides and she picks up her copy of Old Moore's Almanac and reads aloud the predicted disasters. These 'seemed to give her peace, to confirm her sense of order' (p. 84). The boys, too, enjoy the 'ominous pictures', seeing in them the destruction of a world outside which leaves the village still intact.

Granny Trill now takes her customary dinner of cold tea and biscuits, grinding away with her toothless gums. She retells for the boys the story of her father's death, her running wild and her subsequent marriage. Laurie can hardly believe the ancient woman can ever have been young and vital. Nor can he imagine that any man could have planted the enormous tree which grows outside the cottage, but which, says Granny Trill, was planted by her father.

The boys' visit is abruptly terminated when Granny Trill announces she has to 'see to summat'. But she uses no indoor convenience. The boys see her squatting, 'bright-eyed', in the undergrowth: 'Old age might compel her to live in a house, but for comfort she still went to the woods' (p. 87).

Both the grannies, the author says, were types no longer seen. They wore a 'curious, but endearing, uniform' when going out: boots, shawls and bonnets. Granny Trill dresses like this to fetch her snuff, 'her one horrible vice'. This substance exerts an awful fascination over the boys, and provides much amusement for Granny Trill when she sees the results of their taking it. She herself derives ecstatic pleasure from the powder.

Although it is the boys who seem most to visit the old ladies, the girls too pay their respects. On one occasion they are encouraged by their mother to go and see Granny Trill. They deck themselves out in whatever finery is to hand, seeming to Laurie to be 'airborne visions of fairy light' (p. 90). But their visit does not have the intended effect on Granny Trill. She is scandalized by their modern ways, sends them packing and, in a memorable diatribe, warns their mother that 'They'll bring shame on us one of these days', as they take up the airs and graces of their betters – a sentiment Laurie suspects his mother shares.

The two grannies' lives continue to be intimately linked, yet they carefully arrange their lives so that they never see each other: 'Like cold twin stars, linked but divided, they survived by a mutual balance' (p. 91). They are remnants of a bygone age sharing 'the same sense of feudal order, the same rampaging terrible God' (p. 91). Despite never meeting, each is always aware of the other's activities and is acutely affected by them.

One day, Granny Trill breaks her hip. Patiently, she waits for the death that Laurie's mother predicted. As Granny Trill lays dying, Granny Wallon becomes more excited than usual.

At the funeral, attended by most of the village, Granny Wallon remains in the background. But after the coffin has been lowered into the grave, she can contain herself no longer and rants at the graveside that Granny Trill was much younger than she claimed to be. But now, without her ancient rival, Granny Wallon's life loses its purpose: '... she had buried her rival, and now there was no more to do.' Only two weeks later, Granny Wallon dies.

Chapter 6: 'PUBLIC DEATH, PRIVATE MURDER', *pp. 95–111*

This chapter, while still full of finely observed detail, is much darker in tone than the preceding one: it is almost entirely taken up with death and madness, and begins with a story which most of us will find shocking.

The incident the author describes is so 'bloody, raw and sudden' that it is like a shameful family madness that the whole village wishes to cover up.

In the freezing winter weather just before Christmas, a face both 'unknown and familiar' (p. 95) appears in the warm, crowded village pub. The stranger calls everyone by name, buys drinks all round and starts to talk. Originally from the village, he has spent most of his life in New Zealand, where he has made a fortune. The drink makes him boastful, he criticizes the old men for 'the waste of their lives' and the young for 'their dumb contentment' (p. 96). The men and youths drink their free drinks, but say nothing, and begin to steal away.

Late in the evening as the man walks through the silent village to his parents' cottage he is confronted by a group of youths who brutally beat him, empty his pockets and leave him to die. This they do 'for the sake of themselves' (p. 97), as compensation for having had to listen to the man's unpleasant criticism.

The police discover nothing. Though the whole village knows the culprits, there is a total conspiracy of silence. The strength of this desire to keep the secret 'in the family' is shown in the death of the old woman who almost reveals a name in her deathbed rambling; it is as if she deliberately dies rather than risk giving anything away.

Less concealed are 'grief and madness', though they are viewed with muted fascination. The author finds the story of Miss Flynn particularly memorable. This 'off-beat beauty' (p. 99) lives alone and is either reclusive or far too friendly: 'When she saw strangers coming she skipped at the sight of them – into her cellar or into their arms' (p. 99). Her strange beauty fascinates Laurie. Miss Flynn sees her mother's ghost and mixes with strange men; yet Laurie's mother is more sympathetic than critical.

One morning Fred Bates, the milkman, is late with his delivery. He arrives looking shaken and the girls eventually prise the story out of him: he has discovered the naked body of Miss Flynn floating in Jones's pond. Fred Bates becomes an instant celebrity, the women of the village discuss the suicide and Laurie, 'dry with excitement and dread'

(p. 102), rushes off to the pond to gaze with fascination at the place where Miss Flynn drowned. But Fred's celebrity does not last long. The next day he sees another death, after which the superstitious villagers shun him for several years.

In a significant passage (pp. 104–5) the author explains why these events were, and still are, important; they exemplify the state of the village which still maintained close emotional links with a distant past. He describes the village as the latest in a series of connected caves going back to 'ghostly beginnings'. It is a cave that had not yet been stripped of its ancient beliefs by all the influences of modern civilization.

The village people accepted the supernatural as part of their life, and referred to places or ghosts in personal terms, using names of pre-Christian date. Part of this attitude, which helps to explain the first incident in the chapter, was 'an acceptance of violence as a kind of ritual which no one accused or pardoned' (p. 105). To the author as a boy these strange events are exciting but natural: '. . . though dry-mouthed, I was never astonished' (p. 105).

Laurie finds death all around him, and is fascinated by it. In winter, the old people curl up 'like snails'. He tells the story of Mr and Mrs Davies, an old couple who seem to be engaged in a contest of longevity. It is the wife who wins, as her husband takes to his bed. With gruesome detail she recounts to Mrs Lee the onset of her husband's illness, and speculates on the number of people she has known who are now dead.

When Laurie and his brothers are allowed to visit Mr Davies, they see a shrunken old man in a cold, large bed, visibly wasting away. His final wish – that his genitals, his 'doings', be wrapped up in a red silk handkerchief when he is dead – is comically pathetic.

The author describes the valley as sometimes provoking spates of suicides in the 'wet winter days'. But longevity is not unknown. He tells of the seemingly indestructible Joseph and Hannah Brown, a couple absolutely self-sufficient who dote upon each other. Suddenly, they both become ill: '. . . the Authorities were told; the Visiting Spinsters got busy . . .' (p. 110). The capital letters suggest a disapproval of these well-meaning but officious people. The Browns are sent to the Workhouse, an affront to their dignity. But, worse still, they are separated for 'the first time, in all their fifty years . . .' (p. 110) and this kills them. The story demonstrates the sustaining power of love and, at the same time, shows the encroachment of authority into the village: '. . . the kind, killing Authority that arranged it' (p. 111).

Chapter 7: 'MOTHER', *pp. 112–35*

This chapter provides a pen-portrait of the author's mother, an exceptionally important figure in both his life and in *Cider with Rosie*. It is an attempt to explain the unusual qualities that make her such a sympathetic and memorable character.

We learn that his mother was born in 1880 in a village not far from the family's cottage. Laurie's mother accepts the suggestion of noble, but bad, blood somewhere in the family's ancestry with 'shame and pleasure'. She was the only girl in a large family.

As a child she is 'bright and dreamy' (p. 112). Clever, imaginative and mischievous, she is encouraged by her schoolmaster, Mr Jolly, who is touched by this 'freak of intelligence' (p. 113). However, when she is thirteen her mother dies and she has to leave school to look after her brothers and father. With her dreams and aspirations, she is a slapdash housekeeper. Her intelligence and vivacity, though, make her the centre of a lively group of village girls.

Later in her youth she goes into domestic service, the normal course of events for a girl of her social class. It is in the country houses where she works that she glimpses 'luxuries and refinements she could never forget' and acquires 'the idea of the Gentry' which haunts her for the rest of her life. The author tells how, at mealtimes, his mother would sometimes break into a long dreamy description of huge banquets while her children waited for their own meagre meal to be served. This anecdote demonstrates, as do her accounts of glittering social occasions, the fascination that the Gentry hold over Mrs Lee.

Her life as a domestic servant is a hard one, and the author wonders how his mother – 'mischievous, muddle-headed, full of brilliant fancies, half witless' (p. 116) – could have fitted into this strictly hierarchical society.

One explanation may be her beauty, although she herself 'seemed astonished to be noticed'. Laurie Lee gives two stories in his mother's own words which reflect this astonishment. The first is a comical account of meeting an Indian Prince as he is leaving the privy. The second, told in her 'special, morning, dream-telling voice' (p. 117), is about a whole regiment of soldiers saluting the beautiful housemaid in Aldershot on her day off.

She leaves service to help her father run a village pub. Here, in a far from genteel atmosphere of cheap drink and rowdy men, she shows another, tougher, side to her character; she has to throw out the drunks, since her father is too drunk to do it himself, and she is the only person with courage enough to handle the local bully, Pug Sollars. She escapes from this lonely and exhausting life by taking a job as housekeeper to a widower with four children – Laurie's father.

Laurie Lee speculates that she falls in love because this 'rather priggish young man' (p. 121) is so different; he is genteel, has good manners and looks, plays music and is ambitious. He leaves her and she waits thirty years for him to come back. The author says her husband left her because 'she was too honest, too natural for this frightened man'. While she is 'disordered, hysterical, loving' his father wants 'the protective order of an unimpeachable suburbia'. Mrs Lee is altogether too unconventional for her husband.

Their few years together, though, provide her with memories that she feeds on for the rest of her life. But now she must struggle to bring up all the children on the money her husband sends. The problems are exacerbated by 'outbursts of wayward extravagance' (p. 122). Poverty alternates with plenty and she is an inveterate borrower. She is also a great believer in good fortune. Having once been given a small sum of money for a testimonial letter, she sends off hundreds more letters praising the curious products of the time.

Yet despite being 'deserted, debt-ridden, flurried, bewildered' (p. 123) she still has 'an indestructible gaiety which [wells] up like a thermal spring' (p. 123). She changes mood in a second, hitting a child one moment, hugging it the next. She talks incessantly and often makes up funny rhymes about local characters (p. 124). This unpredictability shows itself also in her disregard for time. She is always late for the bus and causes Laurie much embarrassment by sending him to keep it waiting.

Although such escapades encourage the view of her as 'a buffoon' (p. 126), the author remembers his mother as having 'a delicacy of taste, a sensibility, a brightness of spirit' (p. 126) which remain undimmed throughout her life. His first memory of her is as a beautiful young woman, but she quickly becomes 'bent and worn' (p. 126) from her cares. Despite her jumbled knowledge, he says, 'she fed our oafish wits with steady, imperceptible shocks of beauty'; it is for this that he remembers her and because of this his pleasure in beauty always 'pays some brief duty to her' (p. 127).

The Lees' cottage is crammed and cramped, for their mother is an obsessive collector. The house is full of junk, but in one thing in particular – old china – she shows her instinct for beauty. Her hunts for fine pieces and her joy in possessing them shows that they are for her 'magic casements ... opening out on that secret world she knew intuitively but could never visit' (p. 130). But the family's poverty means she can never keep them for long.

Flowers, too, are one of her joys. She has a magic touch: 'One felt she would grow roses from a stick or chair leg ...' (p. 130). The garden is an unplanned riot of colour and perfume, while the kitchen extends this 'outdoor profusion ...'. It is packed with flowers, too, some in the oddest containers.

Her devotion to her husband does not prevent her reminiscing sentimentally about the men who courted her in her youth. Out of these reminiscences we get the delightful story of the blacksmith and the spinster.

The author describes the difficulty he has in trying 'to recapture the presence' of his mother; she is such a bundle of seeming contradictions that it is hard to fix her character precisely. Particularly clear, though, is his memory of her as 'secretly beautiful and alone' (p. 133) when she sits down to the piano after all the children are in bed. Her playing and singing of the songs her husband loved are both beautiful and melancholy. Laurie lies in bed listening, wanting to run and embrace her, but unable to do so.

As she gets older and the children leave home, she grows 'less protesting'. Like Granny Trill she has her own time, and disregards the clock. She hardly ever goes to bed, but falls asleep, fully clothed, upright in a chair. To illustrate both his mother's private sense of time and her desire to care for her children, even as adults, Laurie Lee tells of returning home in the Second World War, at two in the morning. His mother accepts his arrival as something quite ordinary, and Laurie goes to bed, only to be awoken in the middle of the night by his mother bringing him a huge meal.

She spends her last years in 'rustic simplicity', serenely following her own pleasurable pursuits, reading, gardening, writing letters. Then her husband dies. It is 'the death of hope'; her reason for living has gone and she too dies.

Chapter 8: 'WINTER AND SUMMER', *pp. 136–54*

This chapter vividly re-creates the dominant seasons, winter and summer. Through a description of typical days and activities Laurie Lee presents a picture of 'village-winter' and 'village-summer' which substantiates his claim that they 'dominated our every action ... and ordered our lives' (p. 136).

He describes the abrupt arrival of winter, often so sudden that 'the village [has] to be rediscovered' (p. 136). Typically, the cottage's water-pump is frozen, the family drinks boiled ice, and the girls are wrapped in as many clothes as they can find. The milk is frozen in the pails and birds cluster round the windows to be fed.

Laurie and his brothers go out, filling empty tins with smouldering rags to keep their hands warm. The world outside is transformed: 'It was a world of glass, sparkling and motionless', where the air is so sharp it makes the boys sneeze (p. 137).

Laurie and his friends, 'wrapped like Russians', wait for something to do, aimlessly punching each other in the meantime. Suddenly, one boy gallops off, pretending to be a horse. The others follow him through the 'crystal kingdom' of winter, investigating the mysterious changes the cold has brought (p. 138). They go off to help 'Farmer Wells' in his 'warm and voluptuous' cowsheds, where there is such a great contrast to the cold outside.

Having finished their job and collected their rewards, the boys go off. They run into the bully Walt Kerry, who reveals that '"Jones's pond is bearing"' and that the whole village is playing on the ice (p. 140). The boys are ecstatic and rush off to enjoy 'this magic substance' which dumps Laurie on his nose but transforms the clumsy 'dromedary louts' into graceful gliders. Playing on the ice 'Time [is] uncounted; sensations almost sexual'; the boys play until they drop. They stay out far too late and have to collect wood on the way back through the frightening dark. At home, their mother first scolds then pampers them; they thaw out over tea and toast.

At Christmas there is always snow and it is at its thickest in the week before Christmas when Laurie, as a member of the church choir, goes carol singing. The choirboys know exactly the right moment to begin. They meet with their makeshift lanterns and choose a leader. The group of eight sets off and stops at the Squire's house, the customary first call. Here, as they approach the 'Big House' they are particularly nervous – a testimony to the awe in which the Squire is held by the villagers.

They knock at the door and begin to sing with tremulous voices as they stare into the 'huge stone house'. The old Squire himself appears, listens, and gives two shillings, a sum which anyone of any note will want to match. They work their way through the valley, singing more confidently but bickering amongst themselves. They visit all the houses of 'exalted persons' yet never see their audience: 'We sang as it were at the castle walls, and apart from the Squire, who had shown himself to prove that he was still alive, we never expected it otherwise' (p. 146).

After losing Boney, who sets up in lone competition, the boys finish the evening at the house of Joseph the farmer. As they sing their last carol, Christmas is in some way put into perspective for them as the author notes 'two thousand Christmases became real to us . . .' (p. 148).

Summer, too, arrives suddenly, making the world 'unlocked and seething'. In a powerful passage, Laurie Lee describes how, as a boy on these first summer mornings, he would wake to a kaleidoscope of reflections on his bedroom ceiling: 'Watching swans take off from my bedroom ceiling was a regular summer awakening' (p. 149). The phrase is memorable for all its apparent absurdity.

Outside, the world is buzzing in the summer heat. The villagers do not like it, seeing it as 'a kind of punishment' (p. 149). Laurie and his brothers help Mr Brown, the builder, to harness his horse before he takes his family '"Up the hill, for some air"' (p. 150). Then, the boys are at a loss: 'There was nothing to do. Nothing moved or happened at all except summer.' They lie in the grass, luxuriating in the smells and sounds of the summer. They eat sherbert and visit Mr Jones's pond, 'bubbling with life' (p. 151). They meet Sixpence Robinson, who invites them to come and have some fun. There, where all the children's names begin with S, they play with pigeons and have a game of cricket. It is a place of enchantment, 'unspoiled by authority ... where it was summer, in some ways, always'.

The concluding section of the chapter begins with an unusually long sentence which lists some of the sights, sounds, sensations, activities and pastimes of the 'village-summer', when everything is 'twice-brilliant' and smells are 'twice-sharp'. And under the 'melting stars' the boys play 'Fox and Hounds'. In the moonlight they range all over the enchanted valley, chasing the boys who are the quarry: it is a game that makes summer live on in the author's memory and imagination.

Chapter 9: 'SICK BOY', *pp. 155–68*

In this chapter the author writes about his childhood sickness, the first bout of which almost claims him when he is only a day old. He has, he says, the 'rare distinction of having been christened twice' (p. 155). The first time is immediately after his birth. His mother is determined he shall 'enter heaven' and so summons the vicar who baptizes him in the cottage 'from a teacup' (p. 155). But Laurie survives, perhaps through 'some ancestral toughness'. For several months he lies 'inert' and suffers a succession of illnesses. In those days of high infant mortality, his mother can do little but wait and hope.

His closest call comes at the age of eighteen months. His mother is in bed upstairs, having given birth to Laurie's younger brother, Tony, only two days previously. The children are being looked after by Mrs More, a Negress, described as 'a jolly, eye-bulging, voodoo-like creature' (p. 156). Laurie suffers an attack of pneumonia. His sister Dorothy goes upstairs and casually reveals to her mother that Laurie is dead, and is being laid out. His mother staggers downstairs crying '"No one's going to lay out our Laurie!"' (p. 157) and finds him, naked on the table, being sponged by Mrs Moore. She snatches him up, carries him to his cot, and Laurie just pulls through.

Soon afterwards Laurie's sister Frances, his mother's only daughter, dies. Although she was only four years old, the author remembers her watching over him and feels that she gave him her life. His mother grieves daily for her, and thereafter keeps a closer watch over the other children. As Laurie grows, his state of health swings like a pendulum: he alternates between 'a swaggering plumpness' and 'grey-ghosted illness' (p. 158). When he is well he seems quite normal, but when he is ill he disappears for weeks on end. In the summer he sweats in a steaming bed, and in winter freezes in the cold room where the lighted fire signals a serious illness.

The onset of fever brings a return of Laurie's delusions of royalty. He imagines his subjects anxiously awaiting news of his condition, and the messages sent out from his sick-room. The next stage of the illness is delirium: 'by nightfall I was usually raving'. The bed becomes 'a desert of hot wet sand', the walls 'bulge and ripple and roar' and a series of nightmarish 'intangible smiles' descends from the ceiling until Laurie is 'screaming and beating the bed-rails'. It is a vivid evocation of the horrors of illness (p. 159).

His screams bring his sisters running to his bedside. They rearrange him and his bedclothes. Later, in the night, he is 'barely conscious'; he hears himself 'singing, groaning, talking' (p. 160); he sweats and freezes. Solid objects become fluid, the candle casts bizarre shadows and strange voices utter words without meaning.

The night passes slowly, 'as though hot rugs had been stuffed in a clock'. Laurie sleeps, dreams and wakes to find the world 'not a minute older' (p. 160).

Coming out of this delirium 'the real world [seems] suddenly dear'. Everyday sounds are heard more acutely, seem much more precious and Laurie lies 'moved to stupidity by these precious sounds as though ... back from the dead' (p. 162). Then the fever returns, everything goes dark and he is screaming once again in his delirium.

The family grows used to these regular bouts of delirium, and tends to leave Laurie alone to get over them, which he usually does very quickly. He himself does not take his illnesses too seriously, and the thought of death never enters his head. But one night he awakens from delirium to find the whole family clustered anxiously round his bed, 'a mixture of fear and mourning' (p. 163) in their eyes. They whisper their fears to each other. From their manner rather than his own physical feelings Laurie realizes he is very ill indeed.

The girls keep a vigil over him. Next morning the crisis has passed. Laurie has a long convalescence, with visits from schoolfriends and gifts of delicacies. His brother Jack reveals that he has been prayed for at the village church; 'My cup was full, I felt immortal; very few had survived that honour' (p. 164). Laurie takes advantage of his condition and makes the most of his convalescence, successfully inventing an imaginary friend called Archie to avoid taking his hated medicine.

In his convalescence Laurie feels an extraordinary physical transformation; 'my senses were now tuned to such an excruciating awareness that they vibrated to every move of the world, to every shift and subsidence both outdoors and in, as though I were renewing my entire geography' (p. 165).

He lies in bed, delighting in the subtle changes of light and colour 'in a trance of thanks' (p. 166). He is able to 'sense the whole valley by the surfaces of [his] skin', a feeling which makes him feel 'one with the village'.

His mother's care and love make his convalescence a delight, a period in which he feels 'the fatal weakness ... to be always and forever ill' (p. 167).

Laurie's list of childhood illnesses is impressively long. Once, he is even knocked down by a cyclist and lies unconscious for two days –

by which time one of his sisters has fallen in love with the young man on the bicycle. But Laurie's survival is evidence of his toughness. This is a period when children died of illnesses that are now easily cured or prevented. Laurie is 'self-inoculated by all the plagues', and, as a result, survives.

Chapter 10: 'THE UNCLES', *pp. 169–83*

Character studies of four of Laurie's uncles – his mother's brothers – are contained in this chapter. These uncles are important figures for Laurie and his brothers, their heroic stature magnified by the absence of a father in the Lee household. They are heroes whom, writes the author, 'we loved and who were the kings of our youth' (p. 169). Soldiers in the First World War, the uncles provide for Laurie his earliest memories of them as uniformed 'warriors stained with battle', truly 'figures of legend'.

The eldest is Charlie, a slow and quiet man with 'a story-telling voice heavy with Gloucester bass-notes' (p. 170). After the war he works as a forester, living what seems to Laurie a fairy-tale existence in the cottage in the woods. He has had an adventurous past. He has worked as a barman in the rough diamond-mining districts of South Africa, brawling with drunken miners. He disappeared for two years before returning, 'pale and thin and penniless', to Stroud. He is poorly paid, but has great skill as a forester: 'His gestures were caressive yet instinctive with power, and the plants settled ravenously to his touch ...' (p. 172)

The next uncle is Tom, 'a dark, quiet talker, full of hidden strength, who possessed a way with women' (p. 172). Now he lives in a 'small, neat stable-yard' with his wife, working as a coachman. But as a bachelor he had 'suffered almost continuous pursuit' (p. 173) from the girls of the district, which made his sister (Laurie's mother) particularly popular for her value as an intermediary.

For years he 'played a wily game and avoided entanglements', but he comes down to earth after he is relentlessly pursued, but not quite caught, by Effie Mansell. Muddled and thoroughly chastened by this adventure, he marries the girl of his choice and settles down to work, living 'quietly and gratefully' (p. 173) with only his 'solemn winks and knowing convulsions of the brow' to remind them of his 'past grandeur' (p. 174).

Ray is perhaps the most romantic figure of all. He has been 'prospector, dynamiter, buffalo-fighter, and builder of transcontinental railways' (p. 174). Laurie's first sight of him is 'an occasion of memorable suddeness'; he wakes one morning to find in his bed 'a huge and scaly man', his uncle returned from Canada.

Ray is larger than life; 'shining as iron, worn as a rock', with a 'rust-brown face, a gaunt Indian nose'. He is home 'loaded with money and thirst', speaks in a strange accent and is covered in tattoos. He is a 'monstrous toy, a good-natured freak, more exotic than a circus ape' (p. 176) who willingly puts up with the boys' boisterous curiosity.

Sooner or later he goes out on a drinking spree, returning 'wet through, with a dog-like grin', drunkenly sobbing. One such return is even more outrageous than usual, when he crashes his bicycle into the lavatory door.

Because of his money he is pursued by 'toughs' and young women who see him as a very desirable catch. Once he has to hide for three days in the attic from the particularly determined Beatie Burroughs.

The visits of this 'amiable, naïve, sentimental and straightforwardly lustful' man bring a disruption of routine and discipline to the cottage: 'We stayed up late, took liberties, and shared his intoxications . . .' (p. 177). The girls and their mother are by turns outraged and charmed. When his money is spent, he returns to Canada. After a bad accident he is rescued by a Gloucestershire woman, marries her and returns home, so ending 'the pioneer days of that bounding prairie dog' (p. 178).

Uncle Sid is the last described, a figure at once heroic and comical. 'Moody, majestic' (p. 178) is the description given, and the adjectives are fitting. He is majestic in his position as bus driver and former cricketing star, moody in his habit of committing mock-suicide to gain sympathy.

He is first described as 'one of the elite of the bus drivers', manfully wrestling with the primitive giants 'which often ran wild and got their top-decks caught under bridges' (p. 178). This heroic picture is carried over into the description of him as a cricketer with his 'murderous bowling' and his powerful batting, which makes men retreat 'piecemeal to the boundaries'. An old newspaper cutting hoarded by Laurie's mother records that he once scored 126 out of a total of 177 and then took seven wickets for five runs (p. 179).

This is 'the peak of Uncle Sid's glory', although another anecdote shows him knocking down a bully on a village outing, returning to his charabanc and driving home a hero (p. 180).

Sid is similar to his brothers in 'chivalry, temper and drink' (p. 180) and drink is his undoing. His marriage does not prevent him continuing to drink while working as a driver. After suspension without pay he always pretends to commit suicide, thinking that his wife will be more concerned than angry. But he prepares his 'suicides' carefully. Thus, 'If he drowned himself, then the canal was dry – if he jumped down a well, so was that ...' (p. 181).

Finally, he loses his job once and for all. His wife is distraught, fearing he really will commit suicide. Laurie and his brother are sent to look for him. Eventually, they come upon him in the woods, hanging by his braces from a tree. He is in a terrible temper. ' "You've been a bloody long time!" he said' (p. 181).

Chapter 11: 'OUTINGS AND FESTIVALS', *pp. 184–202*

The local celebrations which are the subject of this chapter take place at regular intervals. The Squire is always involved in some way – opening his gardens, distributing gifts, making speeches. He is the central figure in the village.

Peace Day in 1919 is the first festival the author remembers. 'It was a day of magical transformations ...; and I was so young I thought it normal' (p. 184).

The Squire has provided fancy-dress for the villagers, but Laurie's eldest sister, Marjorie, has been busy making herself and others splendid costumes. The five-year-old Poppy Green comes to the house to try on her 'angel's dress'. Laurie is intrigued by her wings and tells her to fly. Naturally, she is unable to do this. Impatient, Laurie pushes her off the mantelpiece. When Poppy has been soothed, the sisters appear in costume, Marjorie as Queen Elizabeth I with Phyllis as her lady-in-waiting. Laurie is overwhelmed by Marjorie, 'who was sixteen and at her most beautiful' (p. 185); Dorothy, as 'Night', is also impressive – 'an apparition of unearthly beauty . . . ; familiar Dorothy had grown far and disturbing' (p. 185).

Jack is Robin Hood, Tony a market girl and Laurie, with his 'squat neck and solid carriage' (p. 186), is given the role of John Bull, a figure whose identity he is unsure of, but whose importance he immediately grasps.

The day is a 'blur of colour'. Laurie's costume falls apart during the procession, and he weeps until he is picked up and deposited on a trolley. The villagers reach the Big House, where they are viewed by the 'wet-eyed' Squire whose aged mother makes a speech from her basket-chair. The gardens are full of strange figures from films and fairy-tales and history, all in various stages of dilapidation after their celebrations.

Village outings are rare. More frequent are the 'tribal wanderings' (p. 188) of whole families as they go out to gather whatever wild fruit or vegetable is in season; 'the free waste of the woods, an unpoliced bounty, which we'd carry back home in bucketfuls' (p. 188).

Often, the family would go for a whole day's outing, usually to visit relations. One such visit, to the house of Uncle Charlie in the woods of Sheepscombe, is described (pp. 188–90). The family steps out early in festive mood, encouraged by their mother who stops to admire the view or keeps their spirits up by teaching the children a rousing hymn.

At Uncle Charlie's house there are welcome refreshments. The two groups of cousins play and fight until they are exhausted. As dusk falls the sleepy family sets off home, drowsily trudging through 'the thick hot darkness', their pace and mood gentle, in contrast to the high spirits of the morning.

Choir outings are usually limited to nearby places easily reached in horse-drawn vehicles. But the arrival of motor-transport, the charabanc, means that they can go further afield. Now the whole village joins in.

One year the outing is to Weston-super-Mare. Laurie and his brothers are too excited and nervous to eat breakfast. They anxiously survey the sky for a clue as to the weather.

Everyone is ready to go, except, of course, their mother, who stays behind washing 'very slowly ... like a duck with all summer to do it' (p. 190). At the pub, the whole village is assembling, loaded with picnics, buckets and spades, bottles of beer; the Squire's old gardener even brings along a basket of pigeons to release from the pier. The chances of good weather are gloomily discussed, the vicar comes to see them off and then the charabancs arrive. Everyone clambers on board, scrambling for seats.

At the last moment Mrs Lee appears and the 'five charabancs, a cherished army' (p. 193), speed off. After a thrilling journey 'wind-borne by motion and pride' the charabancs arrive at the seaside, where 'smells of an invisible ocean [astonish their] land-locked nostrils' (p. 194). The contrast with their own 'deep-ditched valley' amazes them. The men go off to pubs, the women to rest, and the boys to amuse themselves. They revel in the wide-open spaces of sand and mud and then discover the delights of the pier. Here they can sample on the slot-machines 'a whole series of nightmares for a penny' (p. 195). Laurie's favourite is a gruesome representation of a Newgate hanging, which he views over and over again.

As evening falls, the weary revellers re-assemble. The drowsy journey is interrupted for the men to have a last drink. Finally they return to their valley where they 'wake to the smell' of their own houses (p. 196) and Laurie falls asleep with the gaudy seaside images spinning in his head.

The last of the festivals described is The Parochial Church Tea and Annual Entertainment – 'the village's winter treat'. This takes place on Twelfth Night and is 'an orgy of communal gluttony' (p. 196) followed by singers and comic turns from the villagers themselves.

For weeks before everyone rehearses their sketches and songs. On the morning of the event Laurie and Jack go to prepare the school, thus ensuring themselves free entrance. In the evening, the villagers queue and fight their way in. The tables groan with a tempting array of food, but first the villagers must listen to a sentimental and faltering speech from the Squire and grace from the vicar.

Then the eating begins in earnest: 'Cakes, buns, ham, it didn't matter at all, we just worked from one plate to the next' (p. 198). When everyone has eaten enough, they loosen their belts and prepare for the Entertainment. Laurie sweats in anticipation of his turn. He plays the violin in a duet with Eileen Brown. After a shaky start they warm to their task and gain enthusiastic applause from the audience. The rest of the Entertainment is a succession of local characters doing their party pieces. Laurie's sister Marjorie appears as Cinderella, Mrs Pimbury sings a curious song about mushrooms and the Baroness von Hodenburg sings songs about the valley in her outlandish German accent.

The evening is a great success. At home the girls go over their performances. But for the boys the fun is not over; the next day they return to polish off the remains of the feast.

Chapter 12: 'FIRST BITE AT THE APPLE', *pp. 203–15*

This chapter deals with the burgeoning adolescent interest in sex; as suggested in the Synopsis it is the experiences in this chapter which give the book its title.

Laurie's first investigations into the opposite sex take place with Jo, 'so timorous and yet eager to please' (p. 203). Laurie is 'eleven or twelve?'; Jo is younger. Their games take the familiar pattern of him inviting the undemonstrative Jo to a quiet, cool glade on their way home from school. There they play a game in which Laurie, as a doctor, examines Jo, the patient: 'The game was formal and grave in character, its ritual rigidly patterned' (p. 204). Her 'cool limbs' never move while Laurie considers 'in silence all that Jo's acquiescence taught'. Abruptly, the 'consultation' finishes. Jo dresses while Laurie runs home and leaves her to herself.

Eventually, they are discovered. But there is no shame attached: 'very little in our village was secret or shocking . . .' (p. 205). The village is a self-regulating community where 'transgressions [are] dealt with by local opinion'. Punishment for unruly youths is more likely to be 'the fist of the farmer [they] robbed' rather than a visit to the police station. The village has its fair share of crime and perversion, but 'crimes [are] absorbed in the local scene and their punishment confined to the parish' (p. 206) so the problem of sex is 'not one of guilt or concealment but of simple revelation'. Jo has shown the way, but in the confusing turmoil of puberty, that 'tricky wood', Laurie, like all his contemporaries, is uncertain which way to go.

The girls have now come into their own, and are aware of their new power. But they are still accessible. Jo now has been left behind. More attractive are the 'brazen' Bet and the 'provocative' Rosie.

Laurie is full of new energy and sensations, as though 'dipped in hot oil' (p. 207). His body seems to burn, while he and his brother, previously lazy, run and climb trees, getting into 'lathers of exhaustion'. Eventually, though, Rosie Burdock undertakes Laurie's sexual education. It is 'a motionless day of summer' in the haymaking season and Laurie and Jack go to the farm to help. Laurie finds Rosie 'behind a haycock' where she teasingly tells him ' "I got sommat to show ya" ' (p. 208). Laurie is terrified of her and feels 'dry and dripping, icy hot'. She leads him to the shade underneath a hay-wagon, where she shares with him a jar of cider, 'that first long secret drink of golden fire, juice of those valleys and of that time' (p. 209):

Turning to Rosie, Laurie is in a state of tense uncertainty: '. . . her hair was rich as a wild bee's nest and her eyes were full of stings. I did not know what to do about her, nor did I know what not to do.' Rosie makes things easy for him. She moves towards him, 'superbly assured', and pulls him down to her, 'down into her wide green smile and into the deep subaqueous grass' (p. 209).

What happens next is for the reader to interpret since the author remembers 'little, and that little, vaguely'. The image of the hay-wagon floating away on 'motionless tides' gives a clue to the intense, yet indefinable, emotional and physical experience undergone. Afterwards, Laurie and Rosie sit holding hands, drinking more cider and revelling in their physical closeness. As night falls they walk home together. Laurie feels 'like a giant' and performs heroic feats to impress

Rosie. When Rosie has gone her own way, Laurie realizes that his senses seem to have become more acute. He arrives home 'bursting with power and pleasure' and sings rousing hymns outside the house until his brothers arrive to carry him off to bed.

A darker side of village and of adolescent sexuality is seen in the incident which closes the chapter, the 'Brith Wood rape' (p. 211).

Laurie is now one of a 'green-horned gang' of youths, all confused by their 'strength and boredom' (p. 211). In the stable where they meet to play cards and talk about girls, Bill Shepherd one day proposes Lizzy Berkeley as a likely candidate to satisfy their curiosity. She is a dumpy teenager with a touch of religious mania, whose strangeness only makes her seem more suitable.

Bill draws the other boys into his plan. They seem to be able to see it already; 'mad Lizzy and her strumpy, accessible body which we should all of us somehow know ...' (p. 212). The plan, to catch her in the wood as she makes her way home from church, obsesses the boys all week. On Sunday the boys go to the wood and gather at the appointed place. But they soon lose their earlier bravado. As they wait longer and still no one arrives their spirits rise in the hope that they may not after all have to go through with their plan.

Just as they are about to leave they see her approaching. The boys are miserable, but feel they must go ahead. Under the staring eyes of their friends, Bill and Boney approach her. As they attempt to touch her, she hits them and runs away. The boys go home separately and never mention the incident again. As if to emphasize that this is no extraordinary event, the end of the chapter tells us what became of the 'red-fanged ravishers of innocence'; they all marry and live ordinary, respectable lives.

Chapter 13: 'LAST DAYS', *pp. 216–31*

The chapter title, 'Last Days' is apposite. It brings us to the late 1920s, by which time Laurie is twelve, and describes the profound change in the way of life not just of the author's family, but of the whole village.

At the beginning of the author's life the village is tied to the soil and the seasons. It is isolated; the limits of travel are the 'eight miles an hour' of the horse, a limit that has existed 'since the days of the Romans' (p. 216).

All this changes abruptly with the arrival of motor transport; 'the solid-tyred bus climbed the dusty hills and more people came and went' (p. 216). Animals, unused to these forms of transport, die in accidents, as do the aged, 'faced by speeds beyond comprehension'.

The new vehicles are at first rarely seen and transport consists chiefly of a wagonette to Stroud which most villagers disdain to use because of the extortionate fare (a penny). But motor-cars are signs of things to come: 'Soon the village would break, dissolve, and scatter ...' (p. 217). Even so, 'the old life seemed as lusty as ever'. The church still holds an overwhelmingly important place. On Sundays the whole village assembles to hear the vicar. It is a day which follows a typical pattern of 'indulgence and discipline'. Laurie begins his Sundays in 'the usual rush', scrubbing his face, bolting down his breakfast of sausages while trying to learn a prayer for recitation at Sunday School. After Sunday School he goes to church where he is a choirboy.

From his position in the choir-stalls he can survey the hierarchical arrangement of the congregation: the gentry at the front, then 'the Army', followed by 'the rich and settled spinsters' and, finally, 'the wealthier farmers'. The Squire sits by the pulpit, usually dozing through the whole service.

The villagers are solemn and respectful. They go to church out of habit, because it is the thing to do on a Sunday, just as washing is done on a Monday, and also because they are aware of God watching over them, a figure they imagine as like a Squire keeping an eye on his tenants.

After church there are the usual Sunday relaxations; newspapers and 'roasted dinners'. Later, there is Evensong at which attendance is voluntary and the atmosphere much different from the morning: 'The service was almost a reverie, our hymns nocturnal and quiet ... (p. 220).

The year revolves around the great religious festivals, especially for Laurie, since he is a choirboy. Most of all he enjoys Harvest Festival, when the church is bedecked with local produce and becomes 'a horn of plenty, a bursting granary, a vegetable stall, a grotto of bright flowers' (p. 221).

The fact that nearly everyone in the congregation plays some part in the festival means that it cements the village's sense of community and continuity: 'Pride, placation, and the continuity of growth were what we had come to praise' (p. 221).

Radical changes in village life are marked by the death of the Squire. His house is sold, his servants go to work in factories and the estate is broken up. A new freedom of thought and experience is open to young people, who take the opportunities presented despite the vicar's denunciations from the pulpit. And the old people who speak in archaic dialect and dress in a similarly old-fashioned style begin to die off.

The break-up of Laurie's family draws near, too, as the girls begin courting seriously. The first suitor makes his appearance one day when the boiler-works has gone up in a particularly splendid fire. Maurice, Marjorie's boyfriend, is 'followed quite quickly by two other young men, one each for Dorothy and Phyllis' (p. 225).

Now there is a complete change; 'new manners and notions [creep] in' (p. 225) and the young men visit every night, taking turns to kiss their respective girlfriends good night at the kitchen door.

The young men suffer, though, from the enthusiasm and caprices of the girls' mother. One boiling August Sunday she suggests they go for a short walk and a picnic. The young men find themselves conscripted to prepare a picnic 'on a tribal scale' (p. 226). They mutter resentfully under their breath as the whole family sets off, looking like 'a frieze of Greeks bearing gifts to some woodland god' (p. 227).

As the men become more disgruntled, Mrs Lee becomes more ebullient, trying to charm them with 'desperate gaiety' (p. 227). But things go from bad to worse, and the picnic itself is a disaster, as the young men are appalled by the family's habitual disorder and are anxious to be alone with their girlfriends.

When the girls get engaged there is 'a visible increase in tensions' (p. 228). They are in a hurry to leave and set up their own homes: 'Meanwhile, impatience nagged at them all, till in one case it suddenly exploded ...' (p. 228).

One of the girls returns home with her young man. Laurie, doing his homework at the table, picks up snatches of the ensuing argument as mother and sisters gang up on the one who wishes to leave. Laurie and Jack are sent to bed, but rush downstairs when they hear 'the girls screaming, mother howling, and a scuffling and crashing of furniture' (p. 229). They discover the young man pinned to the wall by their mother and sisters: 'He had tried to carry off our willing sister, and we had all of us very near killed him' (p. 229). But family loyalty just as quickly turns to tearful forgiveness.

The girls' engagements, the Squire's death and the improvement in transport all coincide with Laurie's growing awareness of a world outside the valley, where pleasures are 'more anonymous and tasty' (p. 230).

Laurie begins to go to genteel dances in the village. Horses are seen more rarely; musical instruments and ancient gramophones stand unused as people listen to dance bands on the new wireless. The old people begin to die off; Laurie's mother is 'grey now, and a shade more light-headed, talking of mansions she [will] never build' (p. 231).

Laurie himself becomes more solitary and romantic: 'girls were no longer to be treated lightly but were creatures of commanding sadness, and all journeys through the valley were now made alone, with passion in every bush ...' (p. 230). He begins to feel himself special, chosen 'to deliver the world' (p. 231). It is at this time, living 'in a state of raging excitement', that he begins to write the poetry that becomes his vocation as an adult.

Characters

LAURIE

Although *Cider with Rosie* is not a straightforward autobiography, the figure of the narrator is central. Laurie's own development is one of the main themes of the book, and all other characters and incidents are filtered through his consciousness.

The book begins with his arrival, at the age of three, at the cottage. The author effectively conveys the small child's terror at the new surroundings that tower over him: 'The June grass, amongst which I stood, was taller than I, and I wept' (p. 9). This sense of disproportion, of a child's-eye view, is important in this opening chapter.

He is rescued from his terror by his sisters. Throughout the book he draws strength and comfort from the female presence in the household, a presence all the more important in the absence of his father.

We see the young Laurie overcoming his initial timidity and exploring the wider world of people and places as he grows stronger, learns more skills and his curiosity demands satisfaction: 'I measured that first growing year by the widening fields that became visible to me, the new tricks of dressing and getting about with which I gradually became endowed' (p. 13). As he explores 'the paths that lengthened inch by inch with my mounting strength of days' (p. 14) he delights in his discovery of the tactile and visual; the adult author vividly recreates the sensual effect on himself as a child.

Even the end of the war, and all the ensuing distractions, does not halt his explorations for long: 'I soon forgot it and went back to burrowing among the mysteries of indoors and out' (p. 25). Childhood also holds terrors as well as delights: 'the marching of monsters coming in from outside' (p. 28) of his imagination, 'the old men', as well as the comically frightening apparition of Jones's goat (pp. 28–30).

As he gets older Laurie also begins to notice people: 'From the age of five or so I began to grow acquainted with several neighbours' (p. 34). These are village eccentrics who are captured with great economy of description. Their effect on the young boy is to give him an inkling of the diversity of mankind and a sympathy for those who do not fit into the patterns of respectability.

We learn that Laurie, as a child, has repeated bouts of serious illness (pp. 155–68). Indeed, he almost dies at birth and is later given up for dead by Mrs Moore, who is looking after the family. But his sickness is not continuous; he veers between 'a swaggering plumpness' and 'a monotonous return of grey-ghosted illness' (p. 158). These illnesses are attended by bouts of delirium with Laurie raving and imagining horrible visitations.

They also give him an opportunity to indulge in rich fantasy. He imagines himself a king whose health causes grave concern among his subjects (p. 158). This fantasy of a noble birth occurs at other points in the book. In the chapter entitled 'Village School', he writes of a sense of mystery about his birth which makes him feel 'unique and majestic' (p. 54) and he dreams, in 'Grannies in the Wainscot', of commanding a 'parade of grandmas' to satisfy his 'monarch's whim' (p. 88). Later in the book, when Laurie is an adolescent, this theme of the imaginative, inner life is taken up and developed at greater length.

But illness brings its compensation in convalescence, when he is pampered and waited on. He also feels a heightening of the senses, such that 'each morning [he lies] in a trance of thanks' (p. 168). And, rather than being delicate, his survival of the series of illnesses confirms his toughness.

This is shown, too, by his adaptation to life at school. He is initially reluctant and bewildered, 'but after a week [he feels] like a veteran and grew as ruthless as anyone else' (p. 44). His years in the Infants' Room are 'a brief but cosy anarchy' (p. 45), whose only dark point is his summons to the Big Room after experimenting on his friend Vera's head with a lump of wood. He describes himself as a naturally lazy child, 'the fat lord of my nursery life ... idling voluptuously through the milky days' (p. 48).

His contentment is spoilt, though, by his move to the Big Room. But here, too, he rapidly makes the necessary transition, this time from a world of innocence to one 'where one made pacts and split them, made friends and betrayed them' (p. 48). His natural robustness sees him through.

He also displays the first signs of an aptitude for writing. He wins the teacher's approval by faking essays on the lives and habits of otters, about which he knows nothing. He also finds writing poetry easy: 'one wrote a dozen an hour' (p. 56).

But this facility does not set him apart from the village boys. He is a member of the choir and takes part in boyhood games with as much zest as anyone. In 'Winter and Summer' (pp. 136–54) he describes the seasonal games.

In winter he and the rest of the boys go skating on the frozen pond, so absorbed in their play that they lose track of time and play until they drop. There is also the choir's carol-singing, which gives Laurie a glimpse of the life of the valley's aristocracy.

In summer there is cricket or, at night, games of Fox and Hounds which take the boys all over the valley in pursuit of their quarry.

The trip to Weston-super-Mare and the Church Tea, described in 'Outings and Festivals', also emphasize this picture of Laurie as a boy involved in the same pursuits as the others, except, perhaps, more intensely aware of them.

At Weston they charge off to discover the sands: 'We whinnied like horses and charged up and down, every hoof-mark written behind us' (p. 194). His imagination, too, is stimulated by the morbid slot-machines to be found on the pier. At the Church Tea he displays his prowess on the violin, which he has practised in the evenings at home, and eats enormous amounts of food – even returning the next morning to polish off the leftovers.

At home, Laurie does not regret the absence of his father: 'I was perfectly content in this world of women, muddle-headed though it might be ...' (p. 61). He enjoys the affection of his sisters and mother, even though he often goes hungry as he regularly loses out in the scramble with his brothers for food (p. 69).

From his mother he also gets encouragement in his violin-playing and imbibes a sense of beauty: 'she fed our oafish wits with steady, imperceptible shocks of beauty' (p. 126).

The absence of a father is compensated for by the four uncles who are the 'true heroes' of Laurie's childhood. Their manly figures and legendary exploits provide a necessary balance to the predominantly feminine presence in the cottage.

Growing older, Laurie suffers from the confusion and pain of puberty ('First Bite at the Apple', pp. 203–15). Formerly lazy, he now becomes extraordinarily energetic. His confusion is eased by his initiation at the hands of Rosie Burdock, whose forwardness overcomes Laurie's timidity. He feels 'magnificent, fateful' (p. 210) and 'bursting with power and pleasure' (p. 211).

Adolescence also makes Laurie more introspective and solitary: 'journeys through the valley were now made alone, with passion in every bush' (p. 230). He now sees girls in a new light. He becomes much more self-conscious and aware of his own existence: 'voices elected me of all men living and called me to deliver the world' (pp. 230–31).

This adolescent development of his childhood fantasies of noble birth coincides with him writing his first poems 'hour after unmarked hour, imagination scarcely faltering once, rhythm hardly skipping a beat' (p. 231).

MOTHER

The author's mother is such an important figure in the book that a whole chapter is devoted to a portrait of her. This chapter (pp. 112–35) tells us a great deal about her and should be studied with great care. Certain aspects of her character are illustrated in episodes which occur throughout the book and it is important that we should pay attention to the part she plays in other chapters.

The main impression we get of Mrs Lee is one of energetic

confusion, of different emotions struggling for dominance. The author admits the difficulty of presenting any clear account of such a varied character (p. 133):

> Her flowers and songs, her unshaken fidelities, her attempts at order, her relapses into squalor, her near madness, her crying for light, her almost daily weeping for her dead child-daughter, her frisks and gaieties, her fits of screams, her love of man, her hysterical rages, her justice towards each of us children – all these rode my mother and sat on her shoulders like a roosting of ravens and doves.

This volatile mixture of characteristics can partly be explained by her background. Born into poverty in the countryside where *Cider with Rosie* is set, she was an unusually bright child with 'a curious, hungry mind' (p. 112). But her father's objections and the need for her to look after the large family of brothers after her mother's death meant that she could not pursue the education that her schoolmaster thought she deserved.

Her country birth and her early dreams and education are important in any understanding of her character. Of the first the author writes: 'She was after all a country girl; disordered, hysterical, loving ... She lived by the easy laws of the hedgerow, loved the world, and made no plans ...' (p. 121).

The significance of the second two factors can be seen in the pleasure she takes in beauty, whether natural or man-made. Our first view of her in the book is when, 'distracted from duty, seduced by the rich wildness of the garden' (pp. 11–12) she abandons the moving-in to decorate the cottage with a profusion of flowers.

She encourages Laurie's violin-playing and takes great pleasure in his practising (p. 71) and his performance at the Parochial Entertainment (p. 200). She herself sometimes plays the piano and sings.

She is an obsessive collector of old newspapers but also of fine china. It is the latter which affects Laurie more profoundly. Her pleasure in the fine pieces she sometimes briefly possesses is evidence of what he calls 'a delicacy of taste, a sensibility, a brightness of spirit' (p. 126) that she has throughout her life. From her the children received 'imperceptible shocks of beauty' to feed their 'oafish wits' (p. 126).

On the other hand, he says, 'Our Mother was a buffoon, extravagant and romantic, and was never wholly taken seriously' (p. 126). This comic side we see in, for instance, her habitual impracticality, as when she is late for the departure of the charabancs to Weston (p. 190). Her method of stopping when she cycles to the shops in Stroud is memorably eccentric (p. 125).

Her eccentricity shows, too, in the way she looks after the family, 'her panic and innocence, forgetfulness, waste and the creeping tide of debt' (p. 122). Periods of scarcity are followed by extravagant treats (p. 122). Her method of serving breakfast is, to say the least, haphazard: 'a dab on each plate in any old order and then every man for himself' (p. 69). As a result Laurie often goes hungry. The danger of a flood during heavy rain, even though it is not such a real threat, sends her into hysterical panic (pp. 38–9).

Yet she provides her children with great affection and displays strength when it is needed, as when she rises from her child-bed to save Laurie when everyone else has given him up for dead (p. 157). This is the kind of courage we read about in the author's description of his mother, as a young woman, ejecting the local bully from her father's pub (p. 119).

Her emotions are extreme and changeable. She can be tender and sentimental, as when mourning her dead daughter or remembering her suitors before she was married. But she can also be tempestuous to the point of coming to blows, as when her protective feelings for her daughters result in her attacking one of the fiancés in the kitchen (p. 229). Characteristically, she is very soon weeping and kissing him with great affection.

Her constant belief that the husband who has left her will one day return is evidence of the 'unshaken fidelities' Laurie Lee mentions. The author believes that it was the very qualities he admires in his mother that made his father leave her: 'She was too honest, too natural for this frightened man; too remote from his tidy laws' (p. 121).

As she grows older she comes more to resemble the two grannies, Trill and Wallon. The children leave home and her accumulated debris begins to take over the house. Like the grannies, she begins to lose all notion of time: 'She would sleep for an hour, rise and scrub the floor, or go wooding in the middle of the night' (p. 134). When the author returns home during the Second World War, she wakes him near dawn to serve him an enormous meal – his 'dinner' (p. 134). Her death, too, resembles the grannies'. When her husband dies, she has no one to wait for and, therefore, no reason to live.

Laurie Lee's portrait of his mother is full of affection and gratitude. Her idiosyncrasies and contradictions are lovingly recounted, and the picture that is built up is one of a complex but warmhearted woman who succeeded in imparting to her children at least some of her own love of life.

VILLAGERS

There is a wealth of characters in *Cider with Rosie*. Some play a part in one episode, others warrant only a passing mention while others play minor parts throughout the book.

Granny Trill and Granny Wallon belong in the first category. They are the subject of the chapter 'Grannies in the Wainscot' (discussed on pp. 22–4) and little need be said of them here. Their bizarre characters are conveyed by a mixture of direct description and speech. Their language is as archaic as their dress and way of life. Despite their feud, they are very similar types and depend on each other to give meaning to their lives. The relevant chapter should be studied closely for its blend of humour and pathos.

Too many characters are mentioned in *Cider with Rosie* to be discussed here. But it is worth selecting several examples to see how Laurie Lee is able, in the briefest of descriptions, to fix someone in our minds. The selection of village eccentrics in Chapter 2, 'First Names', gives us a good opportunity.

Their nicknames – Cabbage-Stump Charlie, Albert the Devil, Percy-from-Painswick – are such as we are unlikely to forget them. Each is established in an economical description which contains memorable phrases. Albert, for instance, has 'a black beetle's body' and 'soft-boiled eyes of unusual power'; the suggestive images succinctly create an unforgettable picture.

Miss Flynn in Chapter 6, 'Private Death, Public Murder', appears only in the one episode. Yet she, too, is characterized in a few telling phrases and snatches of conversation: 'her long, stone-white and tapering face seemed as cool as a churchyard angel' (p. 99). The simile is striking and apt, given her suicide. Her pallor is conveyed when we are told she looks 'white as a daylight moon'.

The two married couples given as examples of fidelity and longevity – Mr and Mrs Davies and Joseph and Hannah Brown – are also described economically and arrestingly. Mr Davies lies on his deathbed: 'His face was a skull wrapped in yellow paper, pierced by two brilliant holes' (p. 107). While he drifts further towards death his wife seems to get increased energy and enthusiastically describes her husband's ailments to Mrs Lee.

The Browns, 'as absorbed in themselves as lovers, content and self-contained' (p. 108), exemplify long and happy marriage and the end of their story is a sad illustration of what can happen when impersonal authority, although well-meaning, interferes in private affairs. They are, literally, killed by kindness. Their calm contentment is perfectly captured by the author: 'to me they resembled two tawny insects, slow but deft in their movements; a little foraging, some frugal feeding, then any amount of stillness' (p. 109).

Other memorable village characters appear in Chapter 11, taking part in the Parochial Church Tea and Entertainment. There is Major Doreton, the ex-Indian Army officer, who curses the audience 'in English and Urdu' as he struggles with his banjo (p. 200).

There is the extraordinary figure of Baroness von Hodenburg, with her comical German accent, whose appearance 'enshrined all the mystery of art'. These characters appear only once in the book, are briefly but tellingly described, and are then put aside.

SCHOOLFRIENDS AND TEACHERS

Few of Laurie's companions are described in any detail. Many are merely names – Betty Gleed, Clary Hogg – while some appear in several different episodes. Walt Kerry, the bully, appears in the chapter 'Village School' taking the answers to Laurie's sums 'as his tributary right' (p. 55). Later, in 'Winter and Summer', Laurie and friends encounter him in the village where he boastingly reveals, as if it is his doing, that the village pond is frozen. He takes part, too, in the carol singing.

Horace and Boney, the brothers who are 'always fighting everybody and always getting the worst of it' (p. 143) are also involved in the carolling. After a dispute about the quality of his voice, Boney leaves the others and sings alone.

Walt Kerry and Boney are also part of the group which plans the Brith Wood rape. We learn that later Boney is ensnared by a rich widow 'who worked him to death in her bed and barnyard' (p. 215) and that Walt goes to sea before marrying 'into the fish-frying business'.

The most memorable of Laurie's schoolmates is Spadge Hopkins, the unlikely rebel who humiliates Crabby. The overgrown Spadge is a dull, heavy boy who wishes only to escape to the outside world. He is a comically incongruous figure in the small classroom: 'The sight of him squeezed into his tiny desk was worse than a bullock in ballet-shoes' (p. 50).

The girls in Laurie's childhood and youth are presented in rather more detail. In the Infants' Room he is interested in Poppy and Jo, 'limpet chums', and the unfortunate Vera. Laurie feels 'a curious compassion' for the 'lonely, fuzzy and short' girl, a compassion that does not prevent him from conducting an experiment by banging a stick on her head.

In adolescence Laurie first explores sex through games with Jo, 'so timorous yet eager to please' (p. 203). Her acquiescence in his exploration of her body is not enough when he is a little older. Now he is fascinated by Bet and Rosie. Bet, 'big for eleven and shabbily blonde', is outrageously frank: 'For a wine-gum she would have stripped in church' (p. 207). Rosie is 'more devious and sly', but it is she who finally robs Laurie of his innocence. She has 'cat-like eyes and a curling mouth' and a provocative manner. Later she marries a soldier.

The first teacher who makes an impression is the 'beautiful assistant' whom he wistfully remembers 'leaning her bosom against our faces and guiding our wandering fingers' (p. 44). She is followed by 'an opulent widow' whom Laurie embarrasses by asking if she wears a wig.

It is only with Laurie's promotion to the Big Room that a teacher is described in more detail. Here we meet Miss B, nicknamed Crabby. She is a vividly drawn character. Physical details bring her horribly alive. She is 'as physically soothing as a rake', with 'a bunched and punitive little body'. Her restlessness and strictness are conveyed in a list of verbs: 'she spied, she pried, she crouched, she crept, she pounced – she was a terror' (p. 49). But the episode where her authority is humiliatingly broken by Spadge Hopkins's rebellion leaves us feeling almost sorry for her as she sits on top of a cupboard and weeps.

Laurie's last teacher is the more professional Miss Wardley. She wore 'sharp glass jewellery which winked as she walked and she sounded her "gees" like gongs'. Strict without being harsh, Miss Wardley disapproves rather of Laurie's laziness and repeatedly sends him outside to blow his nose.

THE SQUIRE

The Squire is the central figure in village life, around whom everything revolves. He opens his gardens on big occasions, donates costumes for the Peace Day celebrations and money for the Parochial Tea. Many villagers work for him or rent farms from him.

He is a figure of authority, somewhat remote, and we are not given a detailed description of him. Laurie only catches glimpses of him at church or when the choir visits his house, carol singing.

He is an old man with a propensity to tears: he looks at the carol singers with 'moist blind eyes' (p. 144). On Peace Day the village procession reaches his house: 'On the steps of the Manor stood the wet-eyed Squire, already in tears at the sight of us' (p. 187). At the Parochial Church Tea and Entertainment he appears through the curtains to make a speech, again with 'dim, wet eyes' (p. 198). He almost forgets why he is there, and proceeds to make an incoherent speech, breaking off to hide the tears which are about to break out.

At church he takes his place in his pew by the pulpit, but sleeps through most of the service 'like a beaming child' (p. 219). With his death, the old order of the village breaks down.

SISTERS

Laurie's half-sisters, Marjorie, Dorothy and Phyllis, have important roles in the book. When Laurie is very young, they are figures of comfort and protection. As he gets older he sees them more as ideal figures of womanhood.

In the very first chapter they appear to rescue the terrified Laurie, 'brushing off terror with their broad scoldings and affection' (p. 9). They reassure him when he fears he is blind (p. 17) and help him to dress. When their mother is absent they run the household, but in a haphazard fashion: 'Doth giggled helplessly, Phyl wept among the vegetables, and Marjorie would say, when the day was over, "I'd lie down and die, if there was a place to lie down in"' (p. 21). They have their mother's disorganized impulsiveness, and also some of her love of life.

Like their mother, too, they enjoy the horror of the visit from Jones's goat (pp. 28–32) which affects Phyl so strongly that she runs off to have 'hysterics in the pantry' (p. 31).

In Chapter 4, 'The Kitchen', the sisters are described with more detail and differentiation. Collectively, they are 'generous, indulgent, warm-blooded, and dotty'. To Laurie, 'they seemed wrapped as it were in a perpetual bloom, the glamour of their grown-up teens, and expressed for us boys all that women should be in beauty, style and artifice' (p. 61). The eldest, Marjorie, he describes as 'a blonde Aphrodite'. She is 'tall, long-haired and dreamily gentle' (p. 61). For Laurie she is a loving mother-figure, always sympathetic and comforting.

Dorothy is much more volatile, 'a wispy imp, pretty and perilous as a firework'. She is a dangerous attraction for local boys, thrives on thrills and adventures and is the one who brings home the most outrageous gossip.

Phyllis, the youngest, is more delicate and withdrawn, 'a fragile girl, who carried her good looks with an air of apology, being the junior and somewhat shadowed'. Her age sets her apart slightly from the others and she takes special pleasure in looking after the boys.

These portraits are reinforced by the picture of the girls taking part in the Peace Day celebrations ('Outings and Festivals'). Marjorie, now sixteen, appears as Queen Elizabeth I and her beauty and grace are suitably enhanced: 'Tender and proud in her majestic robes, she was the Queen of Heaven' (p. 185). Phyllis, aged thirteen, is her lady-in-waiting 'with finery of her own' (p. 185). Dorothy appears as 'Night', a disguise which suits her more extrovert temperament: 'an apparition of unearthly beauty, a flash of darkness' (p. 185).

Later, the girls go out to work: Marjorie in a milliner's, Dorothy in a cloth-mill and Phyllis in a shoe shop. From their daily trips to town they bring back a rich fund of gossip.

They also acquire suitors who will take them from the closely knit world of the cottage. In 'Last Days' the author describes the courting of the girls. Marjorie has Maurice, 'handsome, curly-haired, a builder of barges', Dorothy has Leslie, a scoutmaster, and Phyllis acquires 'Harold the Bootmaker'. The comedy of their nightly visits is recounted, as is the jealousy of Mrs Lee when one of the girls finally wants to leave home to be married.

As well as direct description, we also get something of the girls' characters from snatches of conversation quoted. A good example of this is in 'The Kitchen' (pp. 74–6) when the girls are gossiping in the evening. Although the speaker is not named, we can tell from the information and the tone of the voice who is speaking.

BROTHERS

Laurie's half-brother Harold is much older than him. He is described as 'handsome, bony and secretive' and as being rather apart from the rest of the family. He is good with his hands and works on a lathe. When the girls acquire their boyfriends he gets 'the infection', too, and brings home a girl for himself.

Of Laurie's two full brothers Jack is older and Tony younger than himself. Jack is 'the sharp one, bright as a knife' who is Laurie's closest companion. His sharpness shows in the way he disappears whenever his mother wants someone to run an errand and, most memorably, in his technique of getting most food at mealtimes (p. 69). At school he is regarded as something of a genius. He is quickly promoted to the Big Room: 'it was agreed that his brains were of such distinction that they absolved him from mortal contacts'.

Like the youngest girl, Tony is set apart from his brothers, 'a brooding, imaginative solitary'. He is wilful and gifted, making up stories, drawing 'like an artist', but refusing to read or write. At school he is 'impervious either to learning or authority' but has an 'outrageous cheekiness' that helps him get away with anything.

FATHER

Laurie's father plays no active part in the book. What little we know about him comes from Laurie's mother, but he is chiefly important because of his absence. His abandonment of wife and family increases the importance of the mother's role in Laurie's life and means that he looks to his uncles for the masculine examples boys need.

Laurie barely knows his father: 'My father left us when I was three, and apart from some rare and fugitive visits he did not live with us again' (p. 60). We learn in Chapters 4 and 6 that he was a handsome and ambitious young man, 'a natural fixer'. He married Laurie's mother after the death of his first wife. His ambition to become a civil servant took him to London where his wife and family did not figure in his plans. The author speculates that his mother was 'too honest, too natural' for him; that his father wanted 'the protective order of an unimpeachable suburbia' (p. 121).

THE UNCLES

All the necessary information about Laurie's uncles is to be found in
the chapter devoted to them. They are particularly important to Laurie
and his brothers, helping to fill the gap left by the desertion of their
father. To some extent, they may be seen as male equivalents of the
author's mother; moody, impulsive and larger than life.

Commentary

STYLE 1

The language and style of *Cider with Rosie* everywhere give evidence that Laurie Lee had been writing poetry long before he came to this book. He uses words as a painter might use paint; adding layer upon layer to create overwhelmingly vivid effects of colour and contrast. With the exception of rhyme, the language of *Cider with Rosie* uses many of the effects we particularly associate with poetry: simile and metaphor, alliteration, rhythm.

Much of the book is concerned with the impact of the world on a child highly receptive to new experience and sensation, and the abundance of information received is admirably conveyed in the many sentences which seem merely to be strings of adjectives, nouns or verbs.

This technique is particularly apparent in the early chapters of the book. His mother decorates the cottage with 'Flowers from the garden, daisies from the bank, cow-parsley, grasses, ferns and leaves...' (p. 11), and we get a clear idea of profusion and variety, while the confusion of Laurie's first day in the cottage is conveyed by 'the ornaments on the unfamiliar floor – the glass fishes, china dogs, shepherds and shepherdesses, bronze horsemen, stopped clocks, barometers, and photographs of bearded men' (p. 11).

Adjectives, in particular, are used lavishly. Laurie's early explorations of 'well-prodded horrors' include '... the crowded, rotting, silent-roaring city of a cat's grub-captured carcass' (p. 14). Each adjective here serves its purpose in building an image of the dead cat crawling with maggots.

Some readers, though, may occasionally find such overabundance of adjectives overdone and tiresome. Sometimes their profusion does seem unnecessary and the second or third adjective seems to add little to what we have been given by the first. But, much more often than not, the effect is successful in giving a vivid image and the feeling of the richness and variety of life.

STYLE 2

Similarly, lists of verbs often convey a confusion or succession of actions. The description of the turmoil of family meals: 'We grabbed and dodged, and passed and snatched, and packed our mouths like pelicans' (p. 72), is a sentence in which the variety of action is augmented by a sharply rising and falling rhythm. The vigilance and busyness of Laurie's mother are captured in another list: 'Eating with one hand, she threw on wood with the other, raked the ashes, and heated the oven, put on a kettle, stirred the pot, and spread out more shirts on the guard' (p. 72).

Laurie, as a young child, discovers '. . . an infinite range of objects and ornaments that folded, fastened, creaked and sighed, opened and shut, tinkled and sang, pinched, scratched, cut, burned, spun, toppled, or fell to pieces' (p. 25). Each verb adds something to the picture of the new and surprising world opening up to him.

Creation of character, too, is helped by such lists of verbs. The best example is in the marvellous description of Crabby, whose frightening energy is brilliantly conveyed: 'she spied, she pried, she crouched, she crept, she pounced – she was a terror' (p. 49). Going into action, 'Crabby coiled, uncoiled, and sprang, and knocked some poor boy sideways'. Both sentences conjure up a physically tense character who takes pleasure in meting out punishment, as a form of release.

The profusion of adjectives in *Cider with Rosie* is matched by the amount of imagery. Again, some may feel that there is rather too much but, again, it is nearly always used to good effect and often provides us with pictures of great clarity and power. There are many examples of simile (the comparison of one thing to another, usually introduced by 'as' or 'like') in the book. In Chapter 2, 'First Light', the deserter who lives in the woods has a face 'red and crinkled, brilliant like fungus' (p. 18), a particularly apt description of a man who seems to Laurie 'a conglomeration of woody things' (p. 18). The isolation of the village in its valley is described in the sentence 'Living down there was like living in a bean-pod' (p. 41). Laurie feeds a calf belonging to Farmer Wells: 'I opened its mouth like a hot wet orchid' (p. 139). Indeed, much of the imagery in *Cider with Rosie* has this immediate, sensuous appeal, using for its comparisons the living things which vividly present themselves to the young Laurie.

Metaphor (when dissimilar things are identified rather than compared) is used even more than simile in *Cider with Rosie*. Each page is crammed with metaphors, many short but vivid. Alone in the terrifyingly long grass at the beginning of the book Laurie cries, lifting his head, 'and the sun hit [him] smartly in the face, like a bully' (p. 9).

The tree planted by Granny Trill's father is described in terms which enhance the ideas of size and age: 'Its roots clutched the slope like a giant hand, holding the hill in place. Its trunk writhed with power, threw off veils of green dust, rose towering into the air, branched into a thousand shaded alleys, became a city for owls and squirrels' (p. 87).

Readers of *Cider with Rosie* will be able to find dozens of examples of imagery in the book, most of them memorable for their remarkable vibrancy and aptness. They will also be able to find other images which seem to be excessive, to add little to our understanding or pleasure. As with adjectives, there is sometimes an excessive use of imagery in the book.

Not all metaphors are short in *Cider with Rosie*. Sometimes Laurie Lee takes an idea and extends it over several sentences or paragraphs. Perhaps the best example of extended metaphor in the book is in the first chapter (pp. 14–15).

The scullery door is a 'harbour mouth' from which Laurie sets out to discover 'rocks and reefs and channels'. Outside is the 'island-garden' while his mother and sisters are 'galleons' leaving 'smells and sounds . . . in their wakes'. The girls are 'full-rigged' with 'white-mast arms' which catch up Laurie 'like a wriggling fish'. The nautical metaphor holds the whole paragraph together and even echoes the first paragraph on page 14 where Laurie compares his explorations to native sailors 'island-hopping across the Pacific'.

Imagery is also essential to Laurie Lee's descriptions of character. One arresting phrase can fix a character unforgettably in our minds. Albert the Devil has 'a black beetle's body' and 'soft-boiled eyes' (p. 35). This last is an unusual and telling metaphor conveying the sinister quality of his glance. Cabbage-Stump Charlie and Percy-from-Painswick are depicted with similar brevity and originality. In such character sketches we see Laurie Lee's sharp eye for detail combined with his great talent for imagery.

Alliteration (the repetition of words beginning with the same sound or letter) is another technique normally associated with poetry which Laurie Lee uses in *Cider with Rosie*. The description of Crabby already quoted is a good example, with the 'p' and 'c' sounds underlining her harsh and unpredictable character.

The langorous, hazy days of summer are evoked by the repetition of 's' and 'z' sounds in Chapter 8: 'The garden, dizzy with scent and bees, burned all over with hot white flowers, each one so blinding an incandescence that it hurt the eyes to look at them' (p. 149).

The spoken language of the villagers is also an important element in the book. The use of conversation helps to give the sense of the particular life lived and also helps in the establishment of character. Granny Trill is memorable as much for her archaic and tetchy language as for any direct description: ' "Well, I'll be bound. That you varmints again?"

"We come on a visit, Gran."

"Just mind them pots then, or I'll cut you to pieces" ' (p. 83).

Chapter 4, 'The Kitchen', ends with almost three pages of direct speech which marvellously captures the confusion of voices in the family and their influence on the half-asleep Laurie. Throughout the book runs the voice of Laurie's mother with its mixture of affection, lamentation and whimsy.

FORM AND STRUCTURE

Students are sometimes confused by the form of *Cider with Rosie*. What kind of book is it? they ask. Is it an autobiography or a novel? Is it fact or fiction? *Cider with Rosie* is none of these things, yet has elements of all of them.

The author himself, in his introductory note, describes the book as 'a recollection of early boyhood' and adds – an important qualification – 'some of the facts may be distorted by time'. In re-creating his childhood days, Laurie Lee is obviously dependent on memory, a faculty which often misleads us. Although most of the book is seen through the child's eyes, the language used is distinctly adult. Indeed, only a gifted and mature writer could hope to recreate the vividness and shock of a child's discovery of the world.

Traditional autobiographies generally begin at a specific point – the author's birth, his parents' marriage, etc. – and relate the story of a life in sequence, until some suitable finishing point is reached.

Cider with Rosie does have obvious autobiographical elements. It begins with Laurie being set down at his new home at the age of three and ends with his discovery of a poetic vocation in late adolescence. In between we are told of schooldays, playmates, the agony of puberty and his first sexual experiences.

Yet, although this autobiographical theme is important in the book, it is not the main one. The book is as much concerned with an evocation of people and places as it is with Laurie's own development.

Much of *Cider with Rosie* is devoted to creating a picture of the vanished village, the world before motor-cars and modern communications. Description of place and atmosphere are essential to the establishment of the book's setting. Characters are sketched as much to show the kind of person who inhabited such a place as for their own sakes.

The book does not have the organized narrative structure – the plot – of a novel. Nor does it show characters developing under the pressure of events, as novels usually do. But the elaboration of memory by imagination *is* characteristic of novels, as are the many details of character and description which make it a pleasure to read.

All this does not mean that *Cider with Rosie* is incoherent or formless. Far from it. Despite consisting, in part, of articles previously published separately in magazines the book does hang together.

This is principally due to the narrator's presence; his point of view leads us through the book, pointing out what we should pay attention to. The lack of a rigid structure allows him to dwell on certain themes or to interpose material where it seems appropriate.

Thus, he can delay a full description of his mother until the middle of the book. By this time we have seen enough of this extraordinary woman to be eager for a more detailed description. Although this chapter can quite profitably be read on its own, enjoyment is enhanced by what we already know, and our further appreciation of the character is enriched by the background Chapter 7 provides.

The first three chapters form a unity, dealing with the young child's explorations until he enters the wider world by going to school. This section ends with a return to the family hearth in Chapter 4.

Chapters 5 and 6 deal mainly with old people whose way of life and beliefs provide a living link with the remote past.

Chapter 8, as its title 'Winter and Summer' suggests, is a contrast of two seasons. Heat and cold are the obvious opposites which hold it together. But there is also a balance between activities, the carol-singing of winter mirroring the game of Fox and Hounds in summer.

Chapters 10 and 11 – 'Outings and Festivals' and 'First Bite at the Apple' – deal with different aspects of the same theme – exploration. The first shows Laurie discovering areas beyond the horizons of the valley, while the second has him making his first discoveries of sex.

As the first chapter showed the family arriving in the village and establishing some order in their cottage, the last ends the book with the break-up of the family as the girls, now much older, leave to set up homes and begin families of their own.

It is not necessary, though, to claim a completely coherent structure for *Cider with Rosie*. Its own terms – 'a recollection of early boyhood' – demand something loose rather than constricted. Memory will not easily, or fruitfully, fit into an easy pattern. Parts of the book – such as Chapter 10, 'The Uncles', or even Chapter 9, 'Sick Boy' – might be put almost anywhere else with little disruption. But, given the mass of detail that memory presented him with, Laurie Lee has made a book that forms a satisfying whole.

THE VILLAGE

Cider with Rosie is a book which re-creates in great detail the way of life of a small village in the years immediately after the First World War. Much of its charm and pleasure comes from the startling and vivid picture which is drawn.

The world described is one that no longer exists and *Cider with Rosie* is an eloquent testimony to a way of life that was centuries old, but died with the arrival of modern communications and technology. Laurie Lee was well placed to write such a testimony: 'The last days of my childhood were also the last days of the village. I belonged to that generation which saw, by chance, the end of a thousand years' life' (p. 216). He was, thus, able to observe both the old way of life and the changes which were to destroy it.

The village to which Laurie Lee was brought, at the age of three, was an isolated community with a rigid social hierarchy and a host of superstitious beliefs.

The village lies in a 'narrow, steep' valley whose shape increases the feeling of isolation and self-sufficiency: 'Living down there was like living in a bean-pod; one could see nothing but the bed one lay in' (p. 41). In the middle of this 'pod', reflecting his position in the village hierarchy, is the Squire's house. The villagers work for the Squire, on farms, or in the cloth-mills of Stroud, the nearest town. The rhythm of life in a community dependent on the land is dictated by the seasons. Both work and play are determined by the recurring festivals which Laurie observes from his position in the church choir: 'From our seats in the choir we watched the year turn: Christmas, Easter and Whitsun, Rogation Sunday and prayers for rain, the Church following the plough very close' (pp. 220–21).

Harvest Festival sees the church festooned with the produce of the valley's farms in a celebration of community and fertility. The

Parochial Church Tea and Annual Entertainment is 'the village's winter treat' (p. 196) while the 'annual Choir Outing' becomes a summer jaunt for the whole village.

The story of Laurie's own development is also told against the backcloth of the changing seasons. As a young child he is amazed by the changes of autumn (pp. 17–18). Later, a whole chapter is devoted to winter and summer and the characteristic pastimes of the two opposing seasons. Christmas sees the annual ritual of the choir's carol-singing while summer is the season of moonlit games ranging over the whole valley.

The villagers' age-old ways of making a living and the valley's physical isolation mean that they still retained a fund of ancient beliefs and superstitions. To the young Laurie 'the yard and the village manifested themselves at first through magic and fear' (p. 28). He describes the village as being one of a series of interconnected caves reaching far back into the past, '. . . a cave whose shadows were cluttered by spirits and laws still vaguely ancestral' (p. 104). The ghosts which inhabited 'each field and hill' were referred to by the older people in 'separate, antique, half-muttered names that were certainly older than Christian' (p. 105).

The presence and reality of the supernatural for the villagers are everywhere apparent in *Cider with Rosie*. Early on there is the appearance of Jones's goat, that 'beast of ancient dream' (p. 30) which strikes terror into the villagers' hearts. There are the various places – Bulls Cross, Hangman's House – associated with terrible events. Fred Bates is at first much in demand after discovering Miss Flynn's body, but is later shunned after witnessing another death. The villagers think he has sinister powers: ' "Twice in two days", the villagers said. "He'll see the Devil next" ' (p. 104).

Village morality, too, was regulated by similar ancient attitudes: 'There was also a frank and unfearful attitude to death, and an acceptance of violence as a kind of ritual which no one accused or pardoned' (p. 105). At one extreme this leads to events such as the brutal murder of the boastful Vincent. His assailants '. . . beat and kicked him for the sake of themselves . . .'. The village accepts his death and closes ranks: 'They belonged to the village and the village looked after them' (p. 98).

Isolation meant that the village had to be self-regulating in matters of morality: 'transgressors were dealt with by local opinion, by silence, lampoons, or nicknames' (p. 205). The author admits that the village was 'no pagan paradise' and had its fair share of 'statutory crime' (p. 206) but believes that the absence of formal authorities was a blessing.

Acceptance of death is seen in the stories of older villagers. When Granny Trill breaks her hip she goes to bed and calmly accepts her fate 'as though some giant authority – Squire, father or God – had ordered her there to receive it' (p. 92). Mr and Mrs Davies warily eye one another as if in a contest of survival. When the man goes first to his deathbed he, too, accepts his fate calmly, while his wife chattily discusses his ailments with Mrs Lee (pp. 107–8).

Village morality allowed, too, for tolerance of unusual behaviour. The numerous eccentrics described in *Cider with Rosie* are not ostracized but accepted. John-Jack is allowed to carry on 'staring gloomily into Wales' and living with the sister who has borne him five children (p. 36). Miss Flynn, the strangely beautiful nymphomaniac, is pitied rather than reviled as a sex maniac.

This tolerance extended also to the sexual explorations of teenagers. Laurie's sex-games with Jo are soon enough discovered, but are not criticized: '. . . we were certainly lucky to live in a village, the landscape abounded with natural instruction which we imitated as best we could; if anyone saw us they laughed their heads off – and there were no magistrates to define us obscene' (p. 205).

The social structure which accompanied such attitudes was hierarchical, almost feudal. Everyone has a fixed place, a fact reflected in the seating arrangements at church where the gentry sit near the front in their own order of birth and wealth: 'All were neatly arranged by protocol, with the Squire up front by the pulpit' (p. 219). The Squire, of course, was the most important figure in this hierarchy. He is the presiding figure at village celebrations, the provider of costumes and cakes, many of the villagers work for him on his estate or in his house. The awe which Laurie and his friends in the choir feel when they approach his house is symptomatic of the villagers' respect. Deference – the respectful acceptance of a higher authority – is the cement which holds this structure together, and its workings can clearly be seen in Laurie's mother. In the chapter devoted to her we are told of the profound effect her days in domestic service had upon her: 'The idea of the Gentry ... stayed to haunt her for the rest of her life' (p. 114). When the family encounters Miss Flynn, Mrs Lee's pity is all the deeper since she thinks Miss Flynn has noble forebears: ' "The poor, poor soul", Mother sighed to herself; "and she half-gentry, too ..." ' (p. 100).

The education provided at the village school is of a kind unlikely to lead the children to question this social organization. The children learn 'nothing abstract or tenuous' (p. 53) but only those things which will fit them for their tasks in life: '... no more than was needed to measure a shed, write out a bill, read a swine-disease warning' (p. 53). The children submit reluctantly to their lessons, longing to be outdoors.

Church too plays an essential part in the village community, as we see in the description given of a typical Sunday (pp. 217–22). The villagers go to church because it is Sunday, 'just as they wash their clothes on Monday', and have an image of God as 'a kind of Squire-archical rent-collector, ever ready to record the tenants' backsliding and to evict them if their dues weren't paid' (p. 219).

THE END OF A WAY OF LIFE

As well as presenting a rich account of the old way of life of an isolated village, *Cider with Rosie* shows us how it coped with the changes imposed by the forces of progress. The author writes that he 'belonged to that generation which saw, by chance, the end of a thousand years' life' (p. 216) and it is this double vision – of the old way and the new – which makes *Cider with Rosie* such a valuable testimony.

Throughout the book time and change are important themes. Laurie Lee emphasizes again and again the continuity of village life, the present's link with a remote past. The village is linked 'to its antic past' and the villagers' superstitions are evidence of 'the blood and beliefs of generations who had been in this valley since the Stone Age'.

Continuity is emphasized by the use of older characters' memories. Laurie's mother fancifully traces her family back to the days of Edward II, while Granny Trill speaks of trees planted by her father, causing Laurie to speculate on the nature of time (p. 87).

Village ancients dress as their grandfathers did and speak in ancient dialect. They 'thee'd and thou'd both man and beast, called young girls "damsels", young boys "squires", old men "masters", the Squire himself "He" . . .' (p. 222).

But the village's self-sufficient life, based on the land and the seasons, cannot resist the developments that take place in the wider world outside. The changes that occur are most apparent in transport and communications, but equally important are the changes in personal and social relationships.

The village's isolation had been a direct result of the means of transport available – the horse: 'His eight miles an hour was the limit of our movements, as it had been since the days of the Romans. That eight miles an hour was life and death, the size of our world, our prison' (p. 216).

The villagers were therefore restricted and the world outside was a mystery: 'The first Choir Outing we ever had was a jaunt in a farm-wagon to Gloucester' (p. 190). Most people preferred to walk the few miles to Stroud rather than pay for a ride on a horse-drawn wagon.

But the arrival of motor-transport heralds the new age. Laurie Lee dramatizes the development: 'Then, to the scream of the horse, the change began' (p. 216). He describes the old folk dying of shock, 'faced by speeds beyond comprehension'.

The villagers' horizons were necessarily broadened; instead of an outing in a horse-drawn wagon to Gloucester, the whole village climbs aboard charabancs and speeds off to Weston-super-Mare. Laurie's Uncle Tom settles down to the old-fashioned job of coachman – working with horses. But his Uncle Sid gets the new-fangled job of bus-driver.

All the influences of the outside world are now brought to bear on the village: 'The sun and moon, which once rose from our hill, rose now from London in the east' (p. 230). The world of Laurie playing the violin in the evenings, of the Parochial Church Tea and Entertainment – of a community which made its own amusement – has gone: 'The flutes and cornets, the gramophones with horns, the wind harps were thrown away – now wireless aerials searched the electric sky for the music of the Savoy Orpheans' (p. 230).

The beliefs and moral standards of the village are now challenged: 'Fragmentation, free thought, and new excitements, came now to intrigue and perplex us' (p. 222). The Church begins to lose its authority; young people marry in registry offices, and Laurie himself is caught reading a daring book – D. H. Lawrence's *Sons and Lovers*.

The death of the Squire is symbolic of the changes taking place: 'With the Squire's hand removed, we fell apart – though we were about to do so anyway' (p. 222). The two most important signs of his power and position – house and estate – are sold off. Servants now take more modern jobs in factories.

The many deaths of old people in *Cider with Rosie* reflect this break in the village's continuity with the past. Their old ways of speech and dress die with them, to be replaced by the fashions Laurie's sisters might see in the shops of Stroud or the patterns of speech they might pick up from the wireless.

The story of Hannah and Joseph Brown also shows how the village's self-regulating morality crumbles in the face of modernity. The devoted couple would prefer to die together in their cottage, but that cannot be: 'the Authorities were told; the Visiting Spinsters got busy; and it was decided they would have to be moved' (p. 110). Of course, the move to the Workhouse kills them. We are left to draw the conclusion that 'killing Authority' will henceforth interfere more and more in such matters, making the village much more like the towns from which it has always been so different. Just as the Squire's death coincides with these momentous changes, so does the break-up of Laurie's own family. As the girls acquire boyfriends and their affections spread from the family home, only their mother will be left, one of the last who still embodies the values of older times.

Glossary

Aigrette: plume of feathers
Aphrodite: Greek goddess of love
Apocalypse: disaster
Apologist: one who defends his opinions by argument
Apostrophe: speech addressed to someone or something not present
Archipelago: a large group of islands
Aromatic: spicy-smelling
Arraigned: called to account
Artifice: decoration
Autopsy: medical examination of a corpse
Backsliding: falling back in faith or morals
Bandeaux: bands for the hair
Bards: singers or poets
Belligerence: aggression
Billhook: hatchet with a curved point
Boers: Dutch colonizers of South Africa
Brassoed: gleaming from Brasso, a metal polish
Brazen: shameless
Brilliants: gems
Brocaded: decorated with brocade, a kind of silk cloth
Buffoon: fool, joker
Burgeoned: grew
Bussed: kissed
Butter muslin: loose-woven cloth

Caliban: monster in Shakespeare's *The Tempest*, enslaved by Prospero
Carbolic: strong soap
Carnage: slaughter
Cartridges: ammunition for a shotgun
Casements: windows
Caste: a social class
Cataleptic: unconscious and paralysed
Charabanc: motor coach
Charnel house: storehouse for human bones
Chastened: moderated, calmed
Chokers: jewelled collars
Clamorous: loud, demanding attention
Collect: short prayer in church service
Comely: attractive, handsome
Conglomeration: jumble of different things
Consumptive: someone suffering from T.B.
Cordite: explosive used in bullets
Crown Derby: a make of china
Cruikshank: nineteenth-century political cartoonist and book-illustrator
Culpable: guilty

Dandy: man who takes great care over dress and appearance

Deferential: submissive, compliant

Diffident: timid, shy

Dilating: expanding, swelling

Diphtheria: infectious throat disease

Discrepancy: variance between facts or feelings

Distemper: common disease of dogs

Dresden: make of china

Dromedary: single-humped camel

Druids: priests of ancient pagan religion in Britain

Earth-closet: outdoor toilet

Elegaic: mournful, reflective

Ermine: white fur (of the stoat)

Escarpment: steep slope

Felon: criminal

Flanders: area of Belgium, scene of many battles in the First World War

Foundered: collapsed

Frugal: thrifty, sparing

Gaitered: wearing a covering over ankle and shoe

Garrulous: talkative

Gaunt: thin

Gibbet: gallows

Gilded: covered in a thin layer of gold

Glutinous: sticky, thick

Goitre: swelling in the throat

Gothic: style of medieval architecture

Grandiose: imposing

Harmonium: a small organ

Home-and-Colonial: name of a chain of shops

Home-Notes: a women's magazine

Incandescence: white heat

Incantation: a chanted spell

Incongruous: not fitting, unsuitable

Inscrutable: inexplicable

Jack-knife: large folding pocket knife

Jazz-debs: fashionable young women of the 1920s

Jets: black stones, worn as jewellery

John Bull: a figure representing the typical Englishman

Kaiser: Emperor of Germany

Kruger: leader of the Boers during the Boer War

Leviathan: gigantic sea-monster. Hence, anything enormous

Limpet: a clinging sea-creature

Linnet: the common finch

Macabre: gruesome, sinister

Megalith: a huge stone prehistoric monument

Melancholia: mental state of misery and depression

Mercury: messenger of the gods

Minim: short musical note

Mnemonics: devices, such as a verse, to aid memory

Mongering: trading

Mons: First World War battlefield

Moot-tree: ancient meeting centre of village

Morose: gloomy, sad

Musk: substance used in making perfume

Nave: main part of a church

Newgate: famous London prison

Oakum. old ropes untwisted and used for making ships watertight

Old Moore's: an almanac containing outrageous predictions

Opulent: rich, luxuriant

Pampas: South American plains

Pantheist: one who identifies God with nature

Paroxysm: a violent fit

Pilloried: placed in stocks and held up to public ridicule

Pince-nez: spectacles without sides, held on the nose by a spring

Placation: appeasing

Pleurisy: inflammation of the lungs

Poke-bonnet: hat with a projecting peak

Porter: a kind of beer

Pre-Raphaelite: in the style of the Victorian group of artists known as the Pre-Raphaelite Brotherhood

Precipitous: steep

Primeval: belonging to the first age

Prom: promenade, a sea-front walk

Purged: cleansed, purified

Puttees: cloth strips wound round the legs from knee to ankle

Quarry: hunted animal

Quartern loaf: four-pound loaf

Rand: gold-mining area of South Africa

Reveries: dreams, fantasies

Righteous: just, upright

Rime: hoar-frost

Ruminative: thoughtful

Rutting: in heat

Sanctuary: a place of refuge

Savoy Orpheans: a popular dance-band of the 1920s

Scrofulous: suffering from a disease causing swelling of the lymphatic glands

Scullery: room for rough kitchen work

Secular: to do with civil, rather than church, life

Sèvres: a make of French porcelain

Shrapnel: fragments of metal from exploded shells

Siege-towers: high, mobile structures used for scaling walls in ancient warfare

Skewbald: marked in white and another colour

Slack: poor-quality coal

Sloes: the wild plum, used in making sloe-gin

Solar plexus: network of nerves behind the stomach

Somnambulant: sleep-walking

Sonorous: rich-sounding

Spode: a make of English porcelain

Stalls: seats for choir in church

Steppe: Russian plains

Stews: brothels

Subpoenaed: summoned to attend in court

Surreptitious: done stealthily or by fraud

Surrogates: substitutes

Syringa: a white shrub

Tableau: a 'living picture', composed of human beings

Taboos: forbidden things

T.B.: tuberculosis, a lung disease

Thermogene: a brand of antiseptic ointment

Timorous: timid, faint-hearted

Torpid: lethargic, sluggish

Translations: great changes

Traps: small, horse-drawn carriages

Tributary: given in acknowledgement of subjection

Tryst: meeting

Turgid: pompous, overblown

Tulle: silken cloth

Unplumbable: unfathomable

Urdu: language of Pakistan

Varmints: vermin

Vestigial: bearing traces of an earlier state

Vestry: room in church where clergy dress

Visionary: one who sees beyond everyday reality

Voluptuous: sensual, full of pleasure

Wainscot: wooden panelling on lower part of a wall

Warrens: rabbit burrows

Wryness: irony, mockery

Yoke: frame of wood for carrying buckets

Ypres: First World War battlefield

Examination Questions

1. Read the following passage, and answer all the questions printed beneath it:

For the first time in my life I was out of the sight of humans. For the first time in my life I was alone in a world whose behaviour I could neither predict nor fathom: a world of birds that squealed, of plants that stank, of insects that sprang about without warning. I was lost and I did not expect to be found again. I put back my head and howled, and the sun hit me smartly on the face, like a bully.

From this daylight nightmare I was wakened, as from many another, by the appearance of my sisters. They came scrambling and calling up the steep rough bank, and parting the long grass found me. Faces of rose, familiar, living; huge shining faces hung up like shields between me and the sky; faces with grins and white teeth (some broken) to be conjured up like genii with a howl, brushing off terror with their broad scoldings and affection. They leaned over me – one, two, three – their mouths smeared with red currants and their hands dripping with juice.

'There, there, it's all right, don't you wail any more. Come down 'ome and we'll stuff you with currants.'

And Marjorie, the eldest, lifted me into her long brown hair, and ran me jogging down the path and through the steep rose-filled garden, and set me down on the cottage doorstep, which was our home, though I couldn't believe it.

That was the day we came to the village, in the summer of the last year of the First World War. To a cottage that stood in a half-acre of garden on a steep bank above a lake; a cottage with three floors and a cellar and a treasure in the walls, with a pump and apple trees, syringa and strawberries, rooks in the chimneys, frogs in the cellar, mushrooms on the ceiling, and all for three and sixpence a week.

(i) Show in detail how Laurie Lee has created a young child's impression of the scene in lines 1–15.

(ii) Give an account of another occasion when the young Laurie Lee was rescued from a nightmare by the appearance of his sisters.

(iii) What is Laurie Lee implying about the condition of the cottage when he speaks of *frogs in the cellar, mushrooms on the ceiling* (lines 26–7)? How do you account for this condition?

2. Read the following passage, and answer all the questions printed beneath it:

So we stumbled and splashed through invisible brooks, followed paths, skirted ominous shadows. We poked bits of stick into piles of old leaves, prodded foxholes, searched the length of the wood. There was nothing there but the fungoid darkness, nothing at all but our fear.

We were about to go home, and gladly enough, when suddenly we saw him. He was standing tiptoe under a great dead oak with his braces around his neck. The elastic noose, looped to the branch above him, made him bob up and down like a puppet. We approached the contorted figure with dread; we saw his baleful eye fixed on us.

Our Uncle Sid was in a terrible temper.

'You've been a bloody long time!' he said.

Uncle Sid never drove any buses again but took a job as a gardener in Sheepscombe. All the uncles now, from their wilder beginnings, had resettled their roots near home – all, that is, save Insurance Fred, whom we lost through prosperity and distance. These men reflected many of Mother's qualities, were foolish, fantastical, moody; but in spite of their follies they remained for me the true heroes of my early life. I think of them still in the image they gave me; they were bards and oracles each; like a ring of squat megaliths on some local hill, bruised by weather and scarred with old glories. They were the horsemen and brawlers of another age, and their lives spoke its long farewell. Spoke, too, of campaigns on desert marches, of Kruger's cannon, and Flanders mud; of a world that still moved at the same pace as Caesar's, and of that Empire greater than his – through which they had fought, sharp-eyed and anonymous, and seen the first outposts crumble . . .

(i) Explain why Laurie and Jack were searching *the wood* (line 3) by night and bring out the humour of line 11.

(ii) Describe Uncle Sid's style as a bus driver and explain why he *never drove any buses again* (line 12).

(iii) At what other activity did Uncle Sid excel? Give evidence of his prowess.

(iv) Explain the reference to *Kruger's cannon, and Flanders mud* (lines 22–3).

(v) They remained for me *the true heroes of my early life* (line 17). Name one of the other uncles and explain why he was one of Laurie Lee's heroes.

(*Oxford Local Examinations, 1979*)

3. Either (*a*) Write a description of the author's mother with special reference to either (i) her eccentricity, or (ii) her affectionate nature.

Or (*b*) What indications were there that the way of life described in *Cider with Rosie* was coming to an end? You should deal with personal relationships as well as changes in environment.

(*Associated Examination Board, 1970*)